DR. STEPHANIE RENAE

Loud Silence

A Memoir of Faith, Healing, and Generational Freedom

Rooted
Wellness

Disclaimer

This memoir contains discussions of childhood trauma, sexual violence, and abuse. While these experiences are shared with honesty, they are written with the intent to shed light on resilience, healing, and faith. Reader discretion is advised.

First edition

This book was professionally typeset on Reedsy.
Find out more at reedsy.com

To My Six Reasons:
Your love gives me the strength and power to move forward every day. You are the light I see when the tunnels are dark. You teach me more than I could ever teach you. Your love gives me life. I love you more than words can convey. I love you forever, I love you always...

To My Grandchildren:
You are proof that God loves me. He loved me so much that He gave me another set of children to love and share life with. My heart will always be your home.

Contents

Acknowledgments   iii

Preface   vi

Before You Begin: Caring for Yourself as You Read   vii

Speak, Black Girls, Speak!   x

Introduction   1

  1 Chapter One: The Weight of Silence   5

  2 Chapter Two: Childhood Stolen   10

  3 Chapter Three: New Life: 23

  4 Chapter Four: Searching for Love—The
     False Security of...   32

  5 Chapter Five: Marriage, Betrayal, and
     Making a Man   41

  6 Chapter Six: Unparented: Healing the
     Wounds of a Mother's...   50

  7 Chapter Seven: The Silence of Motherhood   58

  8 Chapter Eight: Who Worries About the Warriors?   65

  9 Chapter Nine: Learning to Love Myself
     Again—Healing After...   72

10 Chapter Ten: Rebuilding After the
     Storm—Finding Purpose in...   81

11 Chapter Eleven: The Trophy of Tragedy:
     Breaking the...   89

12 Chapter Twelve: No Longer the Villain.   98

13 Chapter Thirteen: Lay It Down and Live:
    The Power of Release   105
14 Chapter Fourteen: Walking in Wholeness
    and Leaving a Legacy   113
15 References   118

Acknowledgments

To My Best Friend, Confidant, and Rider, Quandra:
You have encouraged me more than anyone. Your love and support through the years have been the wind beneath my wings. I am grateful to be doing life with you. I could not have asked God for a better friend. *If you was any bigga... You know!* Thank you for being you!

To My Family:
I treasure you, and thank you for walking this journey with me. There is nothing better than family. Your love and connection have made this life worth living. Thank you for dealing with me through this, staying up late with me, reading page after page as I deleted and rewrote, fussing at me when I needed it, and uplifting me at all times. Thank you. Singing (in harmony as we always do), "We are a family..."

To the Women at The Well:
I cannot tell you how much I appreciate your love and trust. You allow me to guide you through the healing process as we grow together. We have built a family that is safe, loving, and healing. Thank you for showing up over and over again, even when it's hard. Your drive keeps me going.

To My Village:

To everyone who has poured into me, counseled me, mentored me, guided me, protected me, spoken life into me, and took care of me—even when I wanted to be left alone (you know who you are)—I thank you.

To those who have shared a tear, a laugh, or simply their time, your presence has meant more than words can express.

To those who loved me when I was unlovable, who saw my worth when I could not see it for myself, and who helped me gather the scattered pieces of my soul when I was too broken to do it alone—thank you.

To the ones who ushered me into the presence of God when I couldn't find Him in my situation, who carried me when I had no strength to stand, and who reminded me that I was never alone—I am forever grateful.

To the beautiful women who have mothered me, nurtured me, guided me, and corrected me when I needed it—you have shaped me in ways I will never forget. Your wisdom, patience, and unwavering love have been my foundation.

This book is not just my story; it is a testament to the power of community, sisterhood, faith, and love. Every person who has walked with me, held my hand through the darkness, and stood in the gap for me when I could not stand on my own—you are part of this journey.

Heavenly Father:

Thank You for the gift of life. Thank You for seeing me through my trials. I have been kept all this time, and I owe it all to You. Thank You for helping me put my words together in the middle of the night, bottling my tears when they won't stop flowing, wrapping Your arms around me, and reminding me that I am never alone. Thank You for turning my silence into the loud cry that healed my soul. I owe it all to You.

I honor you, I thank you, and I love you.

That's All!

Preface

For so long, I carried my pain in silence. I believed that if I just kept moving, if I kept surviving, I could bury the wounds of my past. But silence does not heal—it suffocates. It deepens wounds, distorts our identity, and convinces us that we are unworthy of love, healing, and freedom.

For years, I asked God why I had to endure so much pain. I now know that my story was never just for me. It was meant to be shared. This book is the testimony of a girl who carried the weight of silence and a woman who found the courage to speak and break free. It is for every Black woman who has suffered in silence while enduring abuse, betrayal, generational trauma, or societal oppression.

As you read my story, you may find pieces of your own story within these pages. I pray you feel seen, validated, and encouraged to begin your own journey toward healing. I do not claim to have all the answers. But I do know this: God restores. He heals. He redeems. And no matter what you have endured, your story is not over.

With love and transparency,
  Dr. Stephanie Renae

Before You Begin: Caring for Yourself as You Read

Disclaimer

This memoir contains discussions of childhood trauma, sexual violence, and abuse. While these experiences are shared with honesty, they are written with the intent to shed light on resilience, healing, and faith. Reader discretion is advised.

This book is raw, honest, and deeply personal. If you have experienced trauma, you may feel triggered, emotional, or even physically affected as you read. Your pain is real. Your emotions are valid. And you are not alone.

As you walk through these pages, I want you to remember:

- You are safe now. The past cannot touch you here.
- You are in control. If something feels overwhelming, you have permission to step away.
- You are loved. Nothing you have been through makes you unworthy of love, healing, or peace.

Before You Begin: Caring for Yourself as You Read

- If at any point this story brings up emotions that feel too heavy, here are ways to pause and center yourself:

- Breathe. Take deep breaths, inhaling through your nose for four seconds, holding for four seconds, and exhaling through your mouth for four seconds. Repeat until you feel calmer.
- Look Around. Name five things you see, four things you hear, three things you can touch, two things you smell, and one thing you can taste. This will bring you back to the present.
- Step Away if You Need To. You do not have to read everything at once. Take breaks when needed.
- Talk to Someone. A trusted friend, counselor, or mentor can help you process what you're feeling.
- Pray. Let God hold the weight of your emotions.

A Prayer for You as You Begin

Lord, I know that healing is not easy. I know that pain lingers, and memories sometimes feel like they are happening all over again. But I also know that You are a God who heals, restores, and redeems. Be with me as I read these words. Remind me that I am safe, loved, and whole in You. Give me strength when the memories feel heavy, and remind me that I am not what happened to me—I am who You say I am. Amen.

Scripture for Comfort

- Psalm 34:18 – "The Lord is close to the brokenhearted and saves those who are crushed in spirit."
- Isaiah 41:10 – "Do not fear, for I am with you; do not be dismayed, for I am your God. I will strengthen you and help you; I will uphold you with my righteous right hand."
- Romans 8:37 – "No, in all these things we are more than

conquerors through Him who loved us."

Final Encouragement

This book reveals pain I have hidden for years, but it is also a story of my healing and survival. If at any point it becomes too much, pause, breathe, and remind yourself—you are still here, you are still standing, and your story is not over.

God is with you. Healing is possible. And you are so much more than what happened to you.

Speak, Black Girls, Speak!

Your silence is loud, but they don't hear you.

They ignore your wailing cries, dismissing them as background noise—lost in the wind that tousles their hair, the change jingling in their pockets, the pages of their books turning past your pain. They have flipped past your suffering, pacifying themselves with words that help them sleep at night.

Meanwhile, the silence of your voice screams like a beating drum. Your silence is loud, but they still don't hear you.

You and your babies bleed out in the streets, in bathrooms, in beds, in closets, in hospitals—while they walk by shaking their heads, offering empty words that dissolve before they ever reach you. They offer senseless solutions wrapped in a culture you are neither able nor allowed to embody. They do not see you. They do not hear you.

But it's time they listen, so...

Speak, Black Girls, Speak!

Turn centuries of loud silence into a roar that cannot be ignored. Make a sound so fierce it forces them to acknowledge you. Let them know that your torture did not disappear when they called you "strong" and "resilient." That your wounds did not heal when they muttered, "I'm sorry." That your anguish did not end when they hash-tagged your loved one's name.

RIP pain? Nah.

They don't hear you, though.

They never have. They build their comfort on your endurance. "You're strong," they say. "You've made it through worse," they say.

But what if you're tired? What if you have nothing left? What if the strength they glorify is really just survival?

Your pieces are scattered, yet your silence is deafening.

But I hear you. Let me heal you. Your children are my children. Your voice is my voice. Your pain is my pain. And we will fight, cry, speak, and heal together.

So, speak, Black Girls, Speak!

Let your words fall to the earth like rain, extinguishing the fire of your pain. Reclaim what was stolen from you. Demand your freedom.

Do not stop until they feel you. Make them hear you.

I hear you. I am listening.

Speak, Black Girl, Speak.

Lovingly,

Dr. Stephanie Renae, The Loud Black Girl

Introduction

Breaking the Silence, Finding Healing

I never thought I would be brave enough to tell my story.

For years, I carried my pain in silence, believing that if I didn't speak about it, maybe it would hurt less. But silence does not erase trauma. It only buries it deeper, where it festers and grows until it threatens to consume you.

The silence inside of me was so loud that it almost took my life. But God wouldn't let it.

A Ministry Born from Pain

I used to ask God, Why me? Why did I have to endure so much trauma, so much betrayal, so much loss? I didn't understand it then, but I do now—my pain was never just about me. God knew I could bear it. And not just bear it—survive it, heal from it, and take what I learned back to help others.

I believe God has given me a ministry for women and youth—to help them heal from the wounds they have been told to keep quiet about. If even one woman or one girl finds hope through my healing process, then every painful moment I have lived will have been worth it.

Collective Healing

I created *The Well Experience* because I knew firsthand what it felt like to carry wounds in silence. Black women and girls have been expected to move through life with resilience while feeling numb inside. We are praised for our strength, but strength without support leads to burnout, isolation, and generational cycles of unhealed trauma.

I wanted to create a space where Black women and girls could breathe—where they could bring their whole selves, without judgment, and receive the support they deserve. *The Well Experience* is a place of restoration, where healing isn't just an individual journey but a collective one. We center Black women's voices, their stories, and their well-being because when one Black woman heals, she brings healing to her family, her community, and the generations that come after her.

Understanding Trauma & Why We Must Speak

Trauma is more than just a painful memory. It is an open wound that does not heal on its own. It changes the way we think, the way we love, and the way we see ourselves.

Trauma whispers lies into our souls:

You are unworthy. You are damaged. You do not deserve to be loved.

For many of us, trauma becomes our identity, not because we want it to be, but because no one ever taught us how to be anything else. I remember being a little girl, crying alone in my room after being hurt by someone who should have protected me. I wanted to scream, but I couldn't. I wanted to tell, but I knew no one would listen.

So, I learned how to be silent. And when trauma is met with silence, it grows. It followed me into my teenage years, shaping

2

the way I saw love. It made me believe that I was only valuable when I was being used. It led me into relationships that weren't healthy because I thought love was something I had to earn.

But trauma is a liar. And the only way to break free from it is to break the silence.

Why I Am Sharing My Story

I am writing this book because someone needs to know they are not alone. Maybe you have spent years carrying the weight of things you were never meant to bear. Maybe you have been told to "just move on" as if healing is that simple. Maybe you have convinced yourself that what happened to you defines you.

I understand. I have been there. But I need you to know—you are more than what happened to you. You are still worthy. You are still loved. And healing is still possible.

What I Hope You Gain from This Book

This is not just my story. This is a testimony of survival, redemption, and God's healing power.

As you read, I pray that you:

- Know your pain is real, but so is your strength.
- Feel safe to confront your own silence. That you are not alone in your healing.
- Recognize that God has never abandoned you. That He sees you, He hears you, and He wants to restore you.
- Find the courage to break your own silence. Because your story matters, too.

I am sharing my truth so that you can begin to walk in yours. And I pray that by the time you turn the last page, you will know—

your silence does not have to define you. God is still writing your story. And healing is still possible.

A Prayer as You Begin Your Healing Journey

Heavenly Father, I come before You with an open heart, knowing that healing is not easy, but with You, it is possible. Lord, for the woman or young girl reading these words, I pray that You wrap her in Your love. Give her strength to confront the pain she has buried. Give her courage to face the wounds she has tried to ignore. And give her peace, knowing that she is not alone. Let this book be a step toward healing, a reminder that she is loved, chosen, and worthy. Lord, remind her that her story is not over and that You are working all things for her good. In Jesus' name, Amen.

1

Chapter One: The Weight of Silence

Silence is never really silent.

It hums beneath the surface, pressing against your chest, filling the spaces where words should be. Silence is heavy, and yet, it moves like a shadow—always following, and never letting go.

For years, I lived with a silence so loud it threatened to consume me. Not the kind of silence that brings peace, but the kind that keeps secrets. The kind that locks pain inside and convinces you that no one will ever understand. I learned silence as a child.

Taught by fear, reinforced by shame, and demanded by survival. I carried it through my teenage years. Buried in my pregnancies, hidden in my relationships, tucked beneath the surface of every smile I forced.

I wore it throughout my marriage. A wife who knew too much but spoke too little. By the time I realized that silence was not my protector, it had already become my prison.

A Childhood Wrapped in Secrets

The first time I understood that silence could be louder than a scream, I was a little girl. I don't remember exactly how old I was, but I remember the feeling of knowing something was wrong but not having the words to explain it, knowing that even if I did have the words, no one would listen.

So I learned to keep things inside. To pretend. To move through life as if nothing was happening, as if I wasn't being hurt by the very people who were supposed to protect me.

I watched the women in my family do the same. I watched my mother cry silently on the couch, tears falling without explanation. I watched my grandmother carry burdens that weren't hers to bear. I watched aunties and cousins navigate pain with quiet resilience—because that's what Black women do, right?

We endure. We survive. We carry it all and say nothing.

And I told myself, *This is just how life is.*

"The Lord is close to the brokenhearted and saves those who are crushed in spirit."
— Psalm 34:18

Silence in Motherhood: The Pain My Children Could Hear

By the time I became a mother, silence was my second language. I thought keeping quiet would protect my daughters. I believed that if I didn't let them see my pain, they wouldn't feel it. But children know. They always know.

My daughters paid attention on the nights I couldn't sleep, when I walked the floor, praying and crying. They felt the weight I carried, even when I smiled through it. They heard the silent cries I thought I had hidden. They didn't need me to say the words. They already knew. And as much as I tried to shield them from my suffering, my silence became their inheritance.

"Train up a child in the way he should go, and when he is old he will not depart from it." — Proverbs 22:6

I was teaching my daughters the same lesson I had learned as a child—that pain is to be endured, not spoken. But that was never God's design.

The Cost of Staying Silent

Silence doesn't make the pain disappear. It only makes it more powerful. I thought staying in an unhealthy marriage was the right thing to do for my family, my children, and the image of what a wife should be. But silence never saves us. It only allows the damage to continue. I lost pieces of myself every time I chose not to speak. I lost time, joy, and the chance to truly heal. Fear stole years from me, while I sat believing that suffering was part of love.

"For God has not given us a spirit of fear, but of power, love, and a sound mind."
— 2 Timothy 1:7

I didn't know it then, but God never called me to suffer in silence. He called me to heal, to break cycles, to speak truth, to live freely.

When Scripture is Misused: "Let the Women Keep Silent"

One of the most damaging lessons I learned as a young girl came not from the world, but from the church. I was taught that women should *"keep silent in the church."*

The Scripture—1 Corinthians 14:34-35—was often quoted to explain why women shouldn't preach, why we shouldn't speak boldly, why our voices didn't belong at the pulpit, in leadership, or even in honest conversations about the pain we carried.

I was told this was God's order. That silence was submission. And that submission was holiness. But the silence I learned in church didn't bring me closer to God—it pushed me further from myself.

As I grew and studied the Word for myself, I began to wrestle with this Scripture. I asked God, *"Is this really what You think of women?"* And the answer was clear in how Jesus lived and loved: No.

Jesus broke the silence of women. He spoke to the woman at the well when others avoided her. He defended the woman caught in adultery when others wanted to stone her. He sat at the table with women, healed them, called them *daughters*, and sent them out with *truth* in their mouths.

The first person to proclaim His resurrection was a woman. That doesn't sound like a God who wants us to be silent. That sounds like a God who wants us to be free.

I don't claim to fully understand Paul's intentions in that letter to the Corinthian church. Maybe he was addressing a cultural issue. Maybe he was responding to disorder in that specific setting. But I know this for sure:

Silencing women is not the heart of God.

I was hurt in many places, but people in the church were responsible for some of the deepest wounds. And my silence allowed that pain to continue unchecked. When I finally found the courage to speak up—about injustice, about harm, about what was happening behind closed church doors—I realized I wasn't just breaking my silence. I was breaking a stronghold.

To the woman reading this who has been silenced in the name of God—hear me:

That was not Him.

God gave you your voice.

He gave you wisdom.

He gave you discernment, power, and purpose.

And He never called you to be voiceless.

He called you to be a vessel.

"There is neither Jew nor Greek, slave nor free, male nor female, for you are all one in Christ Jesus." — Galatians 3:28

Let the silence break here.

Breaking the Silence, Reclaiming My Voice

This book is my way of breaking the silence. This is for the women who have been told to endure instead of escape. For the daughters who grew up in houses full of unspoken pain. For the mothers who are carrying burdens they were never meant to bear. This is for you.

Because your silence does not have to define you. Because your story does not end in brokenness. Because God is still writing your story.

"You shall know the truth, and the truth shall set you free." — John 8:32

And healing begins the moment we decide to tell the truth.

2

Chapter Two: Childhood Stolen

A Stolen Rite of Passage: When Sexual Trauma Shapes Girlhood

For far too many Black girls, sexual trauma has become an unspoken rite of passage. Not by choice or fate, but by the consequences of being unseen, unheard, and unprotected. We do not talk about it enough. We do not name it loudly enough. We have ignored the reality that Black girls are disproportionately affected by sexual violence, often long before they even understand what is happening to their bodies.

According to the National Black Women's Justice Institute, sixty percent of Black girls experience sexual abuse by the age of eighteen. Many are harmed by people they know. Family members. Family friends. Partners of their mothers. People who are supposed to protect them.

This trauma is rarely discussed. It is buried beneath family secrets, masked by silence, and dismissed as something to get over.

We are told:

"Do not wear that."

"Do not sit on his lap."

"Do not tell anyone."

Before we even have language for what is happening, we are trained to carry shame that does not belong to us. Black girlhood is often cut short by the violence of others. Our innocence is stolen, and our silence is demanded. Author Monique Morris, in *Pushout: The Criminalization of Black Girls in Schools*, writes that Black girls are often perceived as older, more sexual, and less innocent than their white peers. This adultification makes it easier for systems and even families to ignore their cries and blame them for their own abuse.

We are over-policed, over-sexualized, and under-protected. The trauma becomes something we carry in silence. We do not tell. We do not cry. We survive. Then we grow up trying to build relationships on top of trauma that was never acknowledged and never healed. We grow up believing that our bodies are for survival, not sacred. That pain is normal. That touch always comes with discomfort. This should never have been our inheritance. This should never have been our introduction to womanhood. Black girls deserve safe childhoods. They deserve to be believed. They deserve to be protected. They deserve to be children.

For a long time, I did not know how to put words to what happened to me. I only knew how it felt. Heavy. Confusing. Shameful. Silent. When I learned how common this pain is among Black girls, I understood something heartbreaking. What happened to me was not rare. It was systemic. It was generational. It was wrong. I was never alone.

I also realized something sacred. Telling my story is not only an act of remembrance. It is an act of rebellion. It is a refusal to carry silence out of loyalty to a family that protected secrets instead of me. It is a refusal to let shame speak louder than truth.

It is a reclaiming of power, voice, and girlhood.

So now, with trembling hands and a steady soul, I open the door to my truth.

Prayer for the Silent Black Girl

You may be sitting in silence, yet I pray you feel the strength to release. I pray that something begins to loosen in you until the shame, the fear, and the silence are gone. I pray that you begin to believe that you are not alone and that healing is your birthright.

Lord,

I lift up every Black woman who carries the wounds of a stolen girlhood. The one who never got to be carefree. The one whose innocence was taken before she even knew what the word meant. God, You saw her. You heard her cries in the dark when no one else did. You counted her tears. You held her pain. Even now, You are restoring what was taken.

To the woman who walks through life with shame that was never hers, remind her that she was never to blame. Remind her that her body is still sacred. Remind her that her soul is still whole. Remind her that her worth is not defined by the ones who harmed her.

Help her release the silence. Let her scream if she needs to. Let her speak her truth without fear. Let her find peace in knowing she is not alone. Heal the places in her that still feel unsafe. Surround her with love that gives and never takes. Remind her that her voice is powerful. Her story is worthy. Her healing is holy. Help her tell her story even if she is afraid. In Your Precious and Holy Name, Amen.

A Broken But Silent Night

The smell of alcohol filled the air before I even saw him. I was nine years old when I learned that the people closest to you can be the ones who hurt you the most. My siblings and I were upstairs in our beds. My mother and her friends were downstairs. She was drinking and laughing, her voice slurred. She and my aunt were too drunk to notice anything strange. They were too far away to hear the way my breath caught in my throat.

I heard footsteps that were slow, careful, and deliberate. I wondered if it was my mother or aunt. We had one bathroom, and it was upstairs, so all of the guests had to come into our space when the drinking had taken its toll. I squeezed my eyes shut and pretended to be asleep as the door creaked open. I thought if I stayed still enough and quiet enough, they would leave. Maybe my mom was checking to see if I was asleep. It would have been the first time, but it was possible.

It was not my mother or my aunt. It seemed the monster that once lived under my bed had come to life. I opened my eyes enough to see his face. Maybe he was lost. Maybe he would figure it out and leave. Maybe he would not see me. But he saw me clearly. He had come looking for me, and he was not leaving until he found what he was looking for.

He leaned in close, his breath thick with liquor, and whispered things I did not understand. Then he put his hands where they never should have been. His hands moved over my body as I lay still, frozen like ice.

"You better not tell." In that moment, silence became my language. I was too afraid to speak. I trembled as tears rolled down my face. A bump in the hallway scared him enough to make him leave the room. He closed my door behind him and went to the bathroom.

Years later, in the stillness of the night, God allowed me to process what had happened. I had buried it deep, believing time had lessened its grip on me. But as I sat there, it all came rushing back. The pain. The confusion. The anger. It felt as though I was reliving it all over again. I needed to write about it, but the words refused to come. Every time I tried, my hands trembled and my thoughts scattered. The weight of my past was too much to put into words. So I wrote it as a metaphor.

That poem later became a part of *Do not Silence My Power: Black Girls Speak*, a collection of poetry written by the women and girls who participated in group therapy sessions at The Well Experience. Through our own healing, I and several phenomenal women guided the group through a writing process that allowed them to heal and release their trauma. In one of the sessions I taught, I encouraged the women to use metaphors for experiences that were hard to put into words. This moment opened a door to healing for women who deserved to be free.

We used storytelling to reclaim our power. African traditions have long embraced metaphor to preserve history, express pain, and teach lessons of resilience. This exercise became a tool for healing, allowing us to place our pain on paper in a way that felt both deeply personal and universally understood.

When I could not write what happened in plain language, I let the metaphor speak for me. Poetry helped me say what trauma had silenced. While teaching a Well Education Family Night (WE Family) on a Tuesday evening at The Well Experience, this poem was born. After walking through a time we remembered being exposed to trauma as a child. We used poetry and metaphors to described an experience we could not find the words to express. The women in WE Family were releasing their stories in safety, and they were healing. I did not plan to write that evening, but the metaphor came to me, and I have to write it down. This is my story.

The Demon in My Room

There's a demon in my room. I did not let it in.

I was asleep peacefully when the seance began.

Just when I thought my death had ended and I could move ahead,

That demon came into my room, and its touch raised my dead

Its hands ran down my body, touching places I kept hidden,

And bringing all my pain to light, although it was forbidden.

The demon told me not to tell and threatened my very being.

It changed the way I saw myself and gave my life new meaning.

My body was cold, frozen like ice, while rivers flowed from my eyes,

The demon didn't care one bit that the moment could be my demise.

"Look at me," the demon said, but I kept my senses closed.

The less I knew about the demon, the less I could expose.

Fear gripped my heart, mind, body, and soul as he continued on his path.

The demon didn't know or care who I'd be in the aftermath.

For in that very moment, a stone consumed my soul,

Predicting the burning, broken glass that would rise from what he stole.

I never told a single soul what the demon did,

But somehow, life revealed the blaze and pulled the shields off what I hid.

For everyone who visited me after that day has felt my pain.

I thought my trauma would sit in silence, but it roared its ugly name.

It reigned like an angry hurricane, consuming without a care,
My Six Reasons have felt the wrath as if they were right there.
So if this demon has visited you, and your life has taken this course.

Join me in standing and taking it back! Let's violently take it by force!
Call that demon by its name, so it knows you are aware,
Of everything it took from you and dared you not to share
That evil spirit did not know the waters deep inside my well
Could cause a flood that smothers demons and breaks their wicked spell.

Come with me where the rivers flow, covering everything along the way.
Join me in taking your power back and claiming your brighter day.

"The Lord is close to the brokenhearted and saves those who are crushed in spirit." —Psalm 34:18

God is near to me in every ache and memory. God holds me when I cannot hold myself. I am not alone, and I am not beyond healing.

I did not know this back then. So, my silence continued.

We Shared Everything

I was tempted to leave this part of my story out, but I decided the silence had held me captive long enough. Generations of pain are locked away in family secrets that are expected to stay hidden behind closed doors. Those chains made me a broken person with the potential to harm others. They were like the sap built up in the tree in Momma's yard, waiting to leak over anything in its path. I am ready to cut the tree down. I have the right to cut it down, and so do you.

I considered leaving this out because it is not only my story but also the story of my childhood best friend. I even considered leaving her out, but it would change the story completely. I am telling this part from my perspective.

We shared everything. We wore the same clothes, got into trouble together, and spent most of our time together. When I was at Momma's house, who was really my grandmother, my best friend and I were inseparable.

We were coming from the bathroom, laughing and snickering as we always did, when we walked past the den that had become a bedroom for a family member.

"Y'all come in here."

We paused. I stood in her shadow and only moved if she did. If she went in, I went in. If she walked away, I walked away.

I walked in behind her, and we both stood in front of him. I did not notice it until he took our hands and made us touch it. I had never seen one before that day. He told us to put our hands around it, and we did. He placed his hand over ours and moved it around. After a few minutes, he put us out, and we went back to my best friend's room. We got in bed and were quiet. We did not talk about it and did not tell a soul. I pushed it to the back of my mind. It crossed my mind from time to time, but I did not give that moment a voice until 2018 when I lay in the hospital unable to move the left side of my body.

The first person I told was my aunt. She asked if I had received a friend request from my great-uncle, who was new to social media. I told her I had received his request, but I would never accept it. She stared at me in confusion and asked why. He was learning to use social media and hoping to connect with family. I told her what he had done to me and my friend. My aunt was shocked and sad. I could see her grieving for me and for the innocence she did not know had been stolen by someone she loved. I noticed her sadness, but I could not focus on it. I felt free. Releasing those few words felt like a lifted weight. I loved that feeling.

The Game of Hide and Seek

My cousin liked to play hide and seek with the younger kids. In his game, he only found me. At first, I thought it was a coincidence and that I was simply bad at hiding. After a while, I realized he was not looking for the others. He was looking for me. When he found me, the game changed.

I wanted to tell someone. I wanted to scream. The silence had already taken root inside me. I was scared and felt helpless. I could not stop him. He would find me, lie on top of me, and push himself inside of me. The pain was unbearable, and I endured it every time. This became a ritual. When he hollered out, "Let us play hide and seek," I knew it meant another uncomfortable moment for me.

When I became brave enough, I stopped playing the game and told him not to touch me. I stayed in the living room on the couch or went outside. I refused to play. Then I thought about who I was leaving to face this. If I stopped playing the game, would my sisters pay. Or even my brother. The game had to end. I started telling my siblings not to play and distracting them so they would do something else. They did not need to know why. They only needed to stop and stay away from him. Bravery came quickly when I was protecting someone else. My fear evolved into anger and a demand for justice, but I still could not gather the strength to tell anyone. I wondered who would believe me and who would care.

"Fear not, for I have redeemed you. I have called you by name. You are mine." —Isaiah 43:1

God knows my name. God claims me fully. I belong to the One who redeems every broken place in me.

What Happens When No One Protects You

The feeling of loss and the lack of protection consumed and overwhelmed me. I wanted to scream and fight, so I did just that. The pain inside turned into anger and rage that I released on people who did not deserve it and on some who did. My body became an open book for men I knew did not love or care about me. I lay there silently as men who never loved me experienced a pleasure that I could not enjoy. I did not know how to enjoy it. I did not even know I was supposed to. No one warned me about men who would see my innocence as an opportunity. No one taught me that love should never cost me my body, my voice, or my worth. No one told me that silence was a curse passed down through generations.

These experiences are not unique to me. Research from Georgetown University's Center on Poverty and Inequality reveals that Black girls are often perceived as less innocent and more adult-like than their white peers. This adultification bias leads to Black girls being seen as needing less protection and nurturing, which makes them more vulnerable to exploitation and less likely to receive support when victimized.

The historical roots of the hypersexualization of Black girls can be traced to slavery. Stereotypes like the Jezebel were used to justify the sexual exploitation of Black women and girls. These harmful narratives still linger today and continue to shape how people view Black girls, often labeling them as promiscuous and less deserving of protection.

I had learned what Black women before me had learned. Pain is something we endure, not something we escape. I also learned something else. Pain that is unspoken never stops moving. If we do not confront it and name it, we pass it down.

"You shall know the truth, and the truth shall set you free." (John 8:32)

Truth is my liberator. I speak what happened to me without shame. Every time I tell the truth, chains fall.

Breaking the Curse

For years, I thought I was surviving. Survival was necessary, but it was not enough. I was carrying generational trauma in my heart, mind, body, and soul. It was controlling me, and keeping quiet felt like it was killing me. Silence shaped my choices and framed my identity. I did not want my daughters to inherit what I refused to heal.

If I did not break the curse or speak my truth, they would carry my wounds as their own. My wounds were spilling over my children, and I did not see it. I chose something different. I chose to name my pain. I chose to speak my truth and be the first in my family to break the silence.

"You intended to harm me, but God intended it for good, to accomplish what is now being done, the saving of many lives." —Genesis 50:20

What was meant to destroy me will become the testimony that delivers others. God turns harm into healing and sorrow into purpose.

Loud Truths I Learned in the Silence

- Silence is not safety. Silence is a slow erosion of the soul.
- Shame is a liar. The blame never belonged to me.
- My body is sacred. No one has the right to trespass against it.
- Telling my story is holy work. My voice is a weapon against generational curses.
- Boundaries are love in action. Protecting myself protects my children.
- Healing requires company. God, therapy, and sisterhood make the journey possible.
- Joy is resistance. I will practice joy as a daily discipline, not as a reward.
- The cycle ends with me. I choose truth, wholeness, and freedom for myself and for my Six Reasons.

Moments of Joy

- Laughter in my kitchen as my daughters danced while we cooked dinner. The music was loud, and our voices were louder. In that moment, love covered my pain.
- A quiet morning prayer walk with my best friend. I felt my breath, and I thanked God for another chance to live healed.
- A sister circle at The Well Experience. We held each other's truth, shared stories, and cried. Then we laughed. The room felt safe, and safety felt like joy.
- Singing at church with my eyes closed and my heart open. The lyrics lifted me, and as the tears flowed, I remembered

that God had been close all along.

- A hug from my grandchild that lingered. Sitting behind me in the same chairs, laying her head on my back while I'm sleeping, and touching my face like its his own. Those arms around my neck feel like a declaration. NaNa is here. NaNa is whole. NaNa is loved.

These moments do not erase what happened. They remind me that even when I taking time to grieve, joy is still mine. They remind me that God is writing a story that refuses to end in sorrow. They remind me that I am free to live, love, and protect the child in me who finally feels safe.

3

Chapter Three: New Life:

Everything Changed

It was the third day of school, seventh grade. I should have been worried about my friends, my classes, and what outfit I would wear the next day. Instead, I walked home carrying moments of silence I had buried but did not yet understand.

When I reached the door, I turned the knob. Locked. I knocked. No answer.

"Mom?" I called again, louder. She could have been sleeping off the night before, so I knocked harder. "Mom!" Still nothing. She knew what time I got out of school. She should have been home.

A voice floated down the walkway from four doors away. In the projects, our doors were only separated by bricks and windows. I could see his face clearly.

"Your mom's gone with my aunt. She said for you to come over here until she gets back."

I hesitated. It sounded true, but something in me felt uneasy. There was nowhere else I could go. So I went. I stepped inside. Everything changed.

A Child Carrying Life

At twelve years old, I became pregnant. I did not understand what that meant at first. I only knew that something was changing. The nausea. The exhaustion. The way my body shifted before my mind could catch up. I had not chosen this. I was carrying life inside me while still trying to understand my own.

Pregnancy was something I had seen on grown women, not little girls who still jumped double-dutch and played kickball. I wanted someone to notice and tell me what was wrong. I wanted someone to hold me and say it would go away. No one did.

I did not say no that day. I did not say yes either. I did not know I had a right to say anything. I lay there in silence, and shame was assigned to me before I could speak.

The Silence of My Mother

I wondered how my mother did not see what was happening to me. She missed the changes in my body, the shift in my spirit, and the flush in my face. For a long time, I believed she did not care. Now I understand that her own wounds shaped her silence.

Unhealed trauma can make it hard to notice or respond to emotional cues, even in those we love. My mother carried a story she had never been allowed to tell. When trauma is all you have known, it becomes the lens through which you see the world, or do not see it at all. Her inability to see my pain was not proof that she did not love me. It was proof that no one had taught her how to recognize and respond to her own.

I thought she would see the change in my movement, hear the shift in my voice, and sense that something had been taken from me. She did not. She never asked, and I never told her. I already knew how silence worked in my family. I carried it alone until it could not be hidden any longer. The morning sickness and my growing belly gave it away. It was time to see a doctor.

> *My mother's first words were, "Oh, Lord. Here we go. Who did you have sex with?" I stared at her without speaking. She asked again, and I told her who it was. Her next question shocked me. "Are you sure? Was there anyone else?" I said no, and she moved on without asking what happened. She told my uncle, and they tried to put money together for an abortion. When those efforts failed, they accepted my reality. No one asked me anything. I felt alone and lost.*

"The Lord is close to the brokenhearted and saves those who are crushed in spirit." —Psalm 34:18

God is not far from your pain. God meets you in the places that hurt and gathers the pieces you cannot hold. You are seen. You are heard. You are not abandoned.

The Stares, the Whispers, the Judgment

As my stomach grew, so did the assumptions. Church ladies whispered and told their children to avoid me. Teachers looked at me with pity. Students acted like pregnancy was contagious. No one asked if I was okay. They decided I was "fast." They said I would lead other children astray. I became another Black girl used to prove a stereotype. All I could see was shame and isolation.

"Do not be afraid, for you will not be put to shame." (Isaiah 54:4)

Do not let shame write your name. Lift your head. Release fear. Refuse to carry what God has already lifted.

My aunt offered to take the baby and raise her as her own, but my grandmother said no. My grandmother, whom I called Momma, stood up for me. She protected me from the harsh words of others. She never asked for my story, but I felt like she knew it all to well. Momma used what she knew to shield me.

Childbirth was the most intense pain I had ever known. At thirteen years old, I brought a baby girl into the world while trying to find my own place in it. I was still a child, yet I had one of my own. I should have been singing in the school choir, running track, going to sleepovers, and worrying about simple things. That was not my reality. I stayed up through the night feeding a newborn and trying to figure out why she wouldn't stop crying. I had helped raise my siblings, but having your own is different. I was afraid of what was to come.

"Fear not, for I have redeemed you. I have called you by name. You are mine." —Isaiah 43:1

I remind myself daily that I belong to God. My name is known. I am redeemed. My child was not a sentence. She was and still is a promise.

What Happens to a Girl Who Never Gets to Be a Girl?
My girlhood had been stripped from me, layer by layer, long before I became pregnant. Silence. Pain. Expectations placed on a child who never got to be one. Many people see Black girls as older than they are and less in need of protection. Bias like this hardens hearts and blocks help. Instead of being nurtured, we are expected to endure. So we endure. We survive. Survival

is not the same as healing.

New Life

I sat at home and looked at my baby girl for the first time. I cried. She was beautiful and full of promise. I started to imagine a life for her that would be better than mine. I was amazed by her presence and terrified of my own. I had no idea how to raise a child of my own. I did not expect support from her father, who denied even touching me. He continued his life. I adapted to mine.

The Longing of My Inner Child

The brokenness in me wanted something. It felt like a need. A longing. I began searching for it. My inner child was looking for love in the wrong places and finding everything else. When love has been absent or unstable, attention can feel like safety, even when it is not.

My inner child was hungry, starving like a child locked outside a warm house. Her nose pressed against the glass, watching as others were fed an abundance of love. She could not even get a taste. She was barefoot in the cold, knocking on doors that never opened. Even if someone had opened a door to real love, she would not have known how to receive it.

She did not want pity. She wanted to be chosen. She wanted to be seen. She wanted to be safe. That broken little girl had no idea what safety should feel like.

I needed to learn that my longing was not about lust. It was about searching for a love I had not known. No one had shown me the difference. I gave away parts of myself to feel whole. No one taught me the language of self-worth. No one handed me a blueprint to wholeness. So I kept searching, mistaking survival for love, attention for safety, and brokenness for belonging. When the world would not feed me love, I tried to earn it with sacrifice. I kept the world's secrets and protected them like they were life itself. I wore open wounds like a badge of honor, not realizing that badge was piercing my heart and stealing pieces of me I could never get back.

No One Told Me

No one warned me about broken men who would see innocence as an opportunity. No one told me that love should never cost me my body. That "being fast" was a label adults used when they did not want to face what happened to us. No one told me my voice mattered and that I could say no and be heard. No one taught me that silence was not my only option.

No one told me that the world would see my body as grown before I even knew what womanhood was. Teachers might call me too loud, not realizing I was hurt and angry and that my voice was the only protection I believed I had. My pain would be questioned before it was comforted.

I did not know that school security guards would watch me more than they watched the boys and say things I was too afraid to report, because who would believe me. I was not warned that walking down the street could feel like a war zone where broken men twice my age felt entitled to my smile, my body, and my attention. My curves would be noticed before my character. Living in the hood meant learning survival before softness, and trauma began to feel normal. I mistook anxiety for personality. The home where I looked for love and safety became the first place I was violated. The noise was so loud that no one could hear my heart begging for help.

No one told me about generational silence. My grandmother,

my mother, and my aunties had survived some of the same things but never said a word. Trauma can dress itself as strength and still bleed through every part of your life. Shame can be inherited and passed down like a precious heirloom.

I watched people take what they had never earned because I did not know I had a choice. I gave away pieces of myself without question. It became a pattern.

These patterns were not only personal. They were historical and systemic. Images and narratives that sexualized Black girls made our pain expected instead of questioned. That lie made apathy easier and intervention rare.

I wanted something different. I would not let my daughter inherit my silence. I would not let pain pretend to be love. As I grew older, I promised that the curse would end with me. I did not know how to raise my baby perfectly, but I knew how to love her fiercely. Sometimes that is the most powerful beginning. I endured judgment with anger and a pride I forced myself to find.

"You intended to harm me, but God intended it for good, to accomplish what is now being done, the saving of many lives." Genesis 50:20

What was meant to break me will build me. What was meant to silence me will send me. God will use my life for healing. My daughter and I will live as evidence of redemption.

Moment of Joy: A Voice in a Tiny Office

I remember the day light found me in a small office at the Urban League. The room was simple. The air was quiet. A light-skinned woman with freckles invited me to sit after arguing

29

with another girl in the program. Her freckles reminded me of Momma. Her voice was soft in a way that felt like safety.

"What do you want to be when you grow up?" she asked.

No one had asked me that in a way that made me feel seen. I heard myself say, "I want to be a good mom." She did not know I already had a child. She didn't flinch. She did not judge.

Her eyes filled with a tenderness I had not known. "You can be a good mom," she said, "and you can be so much more. You are smart. You are brave. You have gifts. The future does not end here, and it certainly goes beyond being a mother. You and your baby can have a beautiful life."

Her words settled in me like a key turning in a locked door. In that tiny office, she spoke life into a girl who had learned to be silent. I walked out feeling taller. I carried her words the way you carry a blessing. They never left me. They still speak.

Loud Truths I Learned in the Silence

- I am not what happened to me. I am what I choose to become.
- My body is not proof of shame. My body is not a debt to be paid.
- My voice is a boundary. When I speak, I protect the girl in me and the girls who come after me.
- Survival kept me alive. Healing is teaching me how to live.
- Love does not require the sacrifice of my worth.
- The cycle ends with me. My daughters will inherit truth, not silence.

Speak Life: I bless my past with compassion. I bless my present with courage. I bless my future with hope. I am a mother who heals. I am a woman who rises. I am a daughter of God, whole and becoming.

4

Chapter Four: Searching for Love—The False Security of Relationships

Love Was Supposed to Save Me

I still believed in fairy tales. Not the horse or the mansion, but the man who would wake me from my slumber. In my fairy tale, Snow White looked like Diana Ross, and the prince looked like LL Cool J, rolling up in a black car like the one from Knight Rider. He would be singing "I Need Love," lean over my bed to kiss me awake, and we would ride into the sunset.

That was my fairy tale. It sounded perfect to me. It did not happen that way.

I thought love would heal my broken heart. If someone chose me, wanted me, and stayed with me, then maybe I would feel whole. Most of the people I met were as wounded as I was. Even when it felt like love, it was hiding unhealed places. I did not know that brokenness cannot heal brokenness. No one told me the emptiness I carried could not be filled by another person. When you have never witnessed love as God intends it, you will settle for whatever looks close to it.

"Above all else, guard your heart, for everything you do flows from it." — Proverbs 4:23

Guarding your heart is not a prison. It is wisdom. It is choosing who and what receives a key. I handed out keys because I was starving for safety. If you have done the same, you are not ruined. You are learning. Post truth at the gate. Post boundaries at the gate. Post God's voice at the gate. Your heart is sacred. Begin again with wisdom, not shame.

My Boyfriend, a Roommate, a Replacement for What Was Missing

He was older than me, and I thought he was a man. His name was Javier. He carried himself with quiet confidence and he knew how to make me feel seen. I let him in. I did not only let him into my home. I let him into my life, into my daughter's life, into my mind, and into my body.

At fourteen years old, I lived like a grown woman. I had a child. I went to school. I worked. I cleaned and cooked. I shared a bed with a man. I thought I was a wife.

Javier was a good young man. He was kind, steady, and protective. He treated me like I was his wife and I felt safer than I had ever felt. I was still a girl. We were playing house.

The Weight of Growing Up Too Fast

Javier saw the chaos in my home and still wanted to stay. Maybe he saw himself in me. Maybe we thought we could rescue each other. He loved me in the only way he knew how. I needed his love to wake up each morning. It was the only thing I felt was real in my life and the one thing that gave me hope. I realized Javier had become my lifeline.

Love built on survival is not love at all. We were not working

33

to heal from our past or present trauma. We provided comfort for each other. That's it. I started to realize how young I was. I wasn't going to school dances, hanging out with friends, or doing anything that fourteen year old girls did. I was coming home to a child and a partner every day.

I did not want to be his partner in struggle for the rest of my life. I wanted to be a teenager. I wanted to laugh with friends, to have crushes that did not turn into commitments, to feel young and free. By the time I realized it, I had already carried adult responsibilities for years, and the only way out was heartbreak.

Research on childhood trauma and attachment shows that when safety is unpredictable, the nervous system can mistake intensity for intimacy. Chaos becomes familiar. The body starts to read volatility as connection. That is why unhealthy love can feel like home. I was living that pattern. It was the only thing in my life that was not hurting me. His love felt like my only truth, and I found rest in it.

"Come to me, all you who are weary and burdened, and I will give you rest." — Matthew 11:28

Jesus speaks to the girl who had to act grown and to the woman she became. Rest is not laziness. Rest is medicine. Lay down the roles that were forced on you. Lay down the fixer. Lay down the pleaser. Lay down the one who always carries the heavy end. Pray this simple prayer. God, I give You the weight I was never built to carry. He will not scold you for being tired. He will hold you.

I still do not understand why my mother allowed her fourteen year old daughter to have a live in boyfriend. I cannot imagine my own children having that experience. That truth hurts. I also

34

see her pain more clearly now. Her choices were shaped by her own survival. That does not erase the harm. It helps me hold the truth with empathy. Generational wounds can blur lines that should be firm.

I believed that love required all of me, even when it cost me pieces of myself. I believed love would hurt me and I should keep forgiving. I believed you do not walk away from someone you love, even when they abuse you, because they still love you and people make mistakes. Those beliefs were not born in me. I inherited them. I stayed in places that were not good for me because that is what I saw.

"Love is patient, love is kind. It does not envy, it does not boast, it is not proud. It does not dishonor others, it is not self seeking, it is not easily angered, it keeps no record of wrongs." — 1 Corinthians 13:4-5

God gave love a shape. When something that calls itself love makes you small, silent, or afraid, it is wearing a mask. Use this scripture like light in a dark room. Let it show you what can stay and what must go. Real love does not require your disappearance to prove your devotion.

Giving Too Much, Expecting Too Little

I married him when I was nineteen. Let's call him Rob. My church held strong traditional values and I believed every word. When the pastor learned Rob and I were having sex, he told us we had to marry. I was not ready. He said it was the only way and that it was what God wanted. We were not rooted in intimacy or understanding. We were infatuated and we were having sex.

"It is better to marry than to burn." I can still hear it. Fear

35

shaped my choices. I wanted to please God, and marriage seemed like the path. There was no proposal. There was no ring. There was a rushed agreement that neither of us was ready for. He promised to love me and care for my children. The way he pursued me convinced me that maybe he was the knight I had been waiting for. I told myself a story that I needed to hear.

He worked hard to win me. He was loving toward my children, generous with gifts, and present in my daily life. I felt like I was first when he was near me. I ignored the signs that told me I was not, and I went heart first into his arms.

My grandmother called me to her prayer house one day. "Are you sure about this, Songbird?" she asked. I answered with my pastor's words. She asked me, "What did God say?" I did not have an answer. I wanted to be a wife so badly that I silenced my gut and my grandmother's wisdom.

"Be alert and of sober mind. Your enemy the devil prowls around like a roaring lion looking for someone to devour." — 1 Peter 5:8

Stay awake. The enemy studies your wounds and sends counter-feits. Counterfeits study your hunger. Alertness is protection, not paranoia. When patterns do not match God's love, trust your discernment and slow down. Ask God for clarity and invite safe people to help you see. What is from God can stand close inspection. You do not have to chase it.

I made space for Rob in my world. I knew somewhere inside that he was not mine in the way a husband should be. I gave him everything. He never fully gave himself to me. I stayed.

He cheated from the beginning. I found the signs and the proof. I endured the abuse. I stayed. I lay awake at night while he was with other women. He called me worthless and pathetic. He told me he could do better and that he could have any woman he wanted. He spent time with women who were supposed to be my friends. He fathered children during our marriage. I stayed.

My self worth sank. I believed his words and blamed myself. I did not feel beautiful. I thought this was my life forever.

"It is for freedom that Christ has set us free. Stand firm, then, and do not let yourselves be burdened again by a yoke of slavery."
— Galatians 5:1

Freedom is holy work. Leaving a toxic situation is not failure. It is faith. Stand in the liberty Christ gave you. Returning to bondage is not loyalty. It is loss. You are allowed to lock the doors you once left open. You are allowed to choose safety over chaos. God calls that obedience.

A Cycle of Searching

One day I told Rob I was going for a walk. I stepped away from the family room and slipped into our bedroom. I sat on the floor in the closet. I closed the doors and let the dark hold me. That closet was my safe place. I talked to God there.

I cried and prayed about the pain of my marriage. I heard the bedroom door open. I heard his voice on the phone. In a few moments I knew this was the end. He told another woman he wanted to be with her and that he planned to leave me. He spoke about me in a way that made tears fall faster. My sobbing gave me away. He opened the closet door and found me there. Shock crossed his face. He hung up the phone. Rage rose in me, but I was not a match for him.

That night I told him I was leaving. He laughed and said I

37

would not make it without him. He might have been right on paper. I did not have work history to prove my skills. I did not have a current driver's license. I had five children and fear. Something was different that day. I was done.

Within two weeks I held a yard sale, packed what I could, and left with five of my children squeezed across the front of an old moving truck. Three sat beside me. Two sat on the floor in front of them. We carried sandwiches, bottles of water, and a printed Map Quest route.

I drove in fear and in prayer. I tried not to draw attention. I asked God to cover us. I did it afraid, and I still did it. I left.

Leaving happens in stages. My body left. My heart tried to stay. Rob lived in my mind. I moved to a new city and met new people, yet the same empty ache followed me. I kept searching for love in people who did not have the ability to love me.

I wanted to feel chosen and safe. I wanted to be seen. I wanted a love that would heal what was broken and restore what had been taken. A man can love me and help me feel safe. He cannot make me love myself. He cannot name me the way God names me. No man should have the power to define a woman's worth. God wanted me to be still and learn His love. My heart was broken and my ears were closed. Pain made me so weak that I could not fight. I couldn't do anything.

"The Lord will fight for you; you need only to be still." — Exodus 14:14

Stillness is not surrender to defeat. Stillness is a strategy. When your strength is gone and your plans have failed, stand still and let God fight for you. Be still long enough to hear which path is dry ground and which path is water. You do not have to perform to be rescued.

I kept reaching for safety in the arms of people who were lost like me. None of them could fill the empty place inside me. Research calls this repetition compulsion. We repeat what hurt us and try to win a different ending. We reach for familiar pain because we hope it will finally feel like love. No matter how we dress it up, it will never become love. It only repeats the wound.

The Truth I Had to Face

I was never unworthy of love. I was never too broken to be loved well. I was searching in places where love did not live.

Real love does not break you. It builds you. The love I needed had been waiting for me in God. Church attendance did not teach me His love. Running to Him with empty hands did. When I had no plan, His love held me. His love did not silence me. His love healed me. His love taught me to love myself and to receive love from others.

"We love because He first loved us." — 1 John 4:19

You were loved first. Your worth was settled before anyone rejected you. Do not love from an empty place. Love from overflow. Let the love of God retrain your body and your mind to recognize safety and goodness. Choose relationships that agree with heaven, not with your history.

"I have set before you life and death, blessings and curses. Now choose life, so that you and your children may live." — Deuteronomy 30:19

Choosing yourself is choosing life. Choosing peace is choosing life. Choosing boundaries is choosing life. Say it with me. I choose life. I choose to live whole so my children can live whole.

Loud Truth I Learned from the Silence

I will no longer gaslight myself into believing my emotions are too much when they are honest responses to mistreatment. I used to shrink, apologize, and question myself to protect a connection. Peace should not require me to abandon myself. I am allowed to feel. I am allowed to set boundaries. I am allowed to walk away when respect is absent.

There is still a part of me that longs for love that is safe. Not perfect, but present. Not performative, but faithful. After betrayal, trust takes time. I still believe there is a love that sees all of me. My softness. My strength. My silence. My scars. A love that sees me and chooses to stay.

Sometimes music says what the heart cannot form into words. "For Anyone" by H.E.R. held up a mirror. I craved what broke me because pain had become my proof of passion. The song helped me name that longing. God has been teaching me that love is not supposed to harm me or make me question my worth. Healing is teaching me that I can be strong and soft. I can be guarded and open. I can be healing and still hopeful.

I did not know real love then. I recognize it now. It sounds like peace. It feels like home. And this time, I know I deserve it.

I will always look for moments of joy. God gives joy in the storm. Sometimes it is small and quiet. Sometimes it is peace that settles the mind. Sometimes it is a child's giggle or a stranger's kindness. It is there. It can be hard to see, but it is still there.

5

Chapter Five: Marriage, Betrayal, and Making a Man

When Marriage Feels Like a Trap Instead of a Covenant

I need to go deeper into marriage. I believe in marriage and still desire this beautiful covenant. When marriage is done right, it blesses us, our children, our community, and the church. When we do not wait for the person God has prepared, that same covenant can unravel all of those blessings.

I thought being married would heal me. I thought it would bring stability, security, and a covering I had never known. I thought it was supposed to be forever, no matter the cost.

Rob was a musician in the church, a man people admired. I noticed how women flocked to him, but I was not impressed. My lack of interest intrigued him. He became determined to pursue me. He learned the songs I would sing and asked if he could play for me. Whatever I requested, he learned. He was talented, and I was honored to have him play while I sang. Still, I did not want a personal connection.

One day he told me he liked me. I laughed and thought, "Boy, please. You are not my type." I told myself that I did not have time for a boy trying hard to look like a man. I was waiting for my king, the man God designed for me, and at the time, I thought I knew who he was supposed to be.

Rob did not fit what I believed God had promised. He persisted. I was longing for attention, touch, and emotional connection. Above all, I wanted a father for my girls.

My longing for love and connection made it appear that Rob was doing all of the right things. It was not long before I was falling for him, even though he did not meet the standards I had set. I was tangled in a web I could not easily leave.

Our pastor noticed the entanglement and decided we needed to marry. When he quoted 1 Corinthians 7:9, and told us marriage was required if we wanted to keep serving, I agreed. I didn't know how to say I wasn't ready. I did not need a wedding. I needed healing. I needed freedom from the beliefs I had built about men and what would make me happy. I knew I was not ready to be a wife, and I knew Rob was not ready to be a husband.

But I did not say it. I followed the plan and married a man I barely knew so we could be physical without guilt and continue working in the church. That is why we were told to get married. We were visible, and the pastor did not want our behavior to make the church look bad. Whether we had healing, wholeness, or even true affection for each other seemed less important than protecting an image. It became about reputation, not transformation.

This pressure happens in church spaces more than we are willing to admit. In some church cultures, urgency can replace discernment, and performance can overshadow discipleship. Couples are pushed toward a wedding instead of pastoral care, premarital counseling, and spiritual formation. The altar becomes a stage rather than a place of truth, repentance, and preparation. When we treat marriage as the fix for desire or appearance, people carry private wounds into a public covenant. The cost is heavy.

I believed that if I loved enough, prayed enough, and endured enough, our marriage would be blessed. It was not. Rob was unfaithful from the beginning. He had not released the women he entertained before me. When I brought my concerns to my pastor, Rob denied them. Even with clear evidence, I was told to pray and make the marriage work. So I stayed. I prayed. I tried to hold a broken thing together with my bare hands while depression consumed me.

I wanted our marriage to work because I did not want to disappoint the church. I wanted to say my daughters had a father. I wanted us to heal, to grow, to be the couple people admired. But marriage is not a cure for brokenness. Love cannot live on hope alone. The bondage I endured under the banner of marriage did not help the church. It harmed me, my children, and the witness of the people who loved us. The worship leader who once sang under anointing now moved through services with a quiet ache. I was dying inside.

"The Lord is close to the brokenhearted and saves those who are crushed in spirit." — Psalm 34:18

God is not distant from your ache. He is near to the breath you can barely catch. Your tears are not evidence of failure. They are prayers He understands. He does not despise your weakness. He draws close to it and calls you worthy of rescue.

I needed healing and freedom. Rob needed healing and freedom. We needed shepherds who would walk us through deliverance and accountability, not only into a ceremony. When the church becomes performative, the people suffer. The Gospel invites transformation. Performance only requires appearance.

The Church Saw the Gifts, Not the Man

Rob's gift drew people. His skill filled rooms. People praised what he could do. Few confronted who he was becoming. Infidelity, dishonor, and lies went unchallenged because the sound was good on Sunday. We gave our gifts and the church shouted. It looked right. It felt powerful. But I needed someone to see the woman behind the microphone who was bleeding. I needed someone to care that the man behind the instrument was not leading at home. In some spaces, talent becomes currency and character becomes optional. The silence around sin became my burden to carry.

The Pain That Does Not Leave

There is a particular pain in knowing your husband has been with another woman. It steals sleep and asks cruel questions about your worth. I hid it until the private wounds became public. The women were not strangers. They sat in the pews and stood near me in the choir. They lived in my community. I could not escape the whispers. My children heard them. My family heard them. Shame tried to build a home in me. Still, I stayed, because I thought that is what a good wife does.

"Love is patient, love is kind. It does not envy, it does not boast, it is not proud. It does not dishonor others, it is not self-seeking, it is not easily angered, it keeps no record of wrongs." — 1 Corinthians 13:4–5

Love is patient, but it is not permissive of harm. Love is kind, and kindness includes truth and boundaries. Love does not dishonor. If a relationship consistently dishonors your body, your mind, or your calling, it is not love. Holy love tells the truth, protects what is sacred, and refuses to hide you behind someone else's sin.

This was not love. This was suffering under a marriage that had already broken.

When Love Becomes Labor

Rob and I had three children together. I became the proud mother of six beautiful daughters. I once prayed for a son because Rob wanted one so badly. That was not God's plan for me, and I am at peace with that. My girls remain the most beautiful part of my story.

The first child Rob fathered with another woman during our marriage was a girl. The betrayal cut deep, yet I convinced myself I was doing right by forgiving and staying. I encouraged him to show up for his daughter. I believed no child should carry the consequence of adult choices. I went with him to meet her. I opened my heart and my home. I thought if I mothered the child he had outside our marriage, he would finally see the depth of my love and choose faithfulness. I believed my sacrifice would transform him.

When her mother faced challenges, I helped bring his daughter into our home. I mothered her because she needed care, and mothering brings my heart joy. I wanted to prove that our family could still stand. It did not work. He entertained another woman while I cared for our children and his child. By the time I finally let go, Rob had fathered four children outside our marriage. I sacrificed, forgave, and believed while he repeated the same betrayal. My behavior could not change him.

45

Change is inner work. It looks like repentance, truth-telling, therapy, accountability, spiritual formation, and consistent fruit over time. It is not tears today and the same habits tomorrow. It is not promises without practice. Transformation is a choice that belongs to the person who needs to change. You cannot do it for them.

The Silent Suffering of Black Women in Marriage

For generations, Black women have been expected to endure. Our grandmothers stayed. Our mothers stayed. We learned to carry pain quietly and to put our needs last. This is not only personal. It is historical. Enslaved women had no agency over their bodies, marriages, or children. After slavery, the expectation to bear pain without complaint still shadowed our homes and churches. The legacy lingers in the pressure to hold it all together at any cost.

"Come to me, all you who are weary and burdened, and I will give you rest." — Matthew 11:28

Rest is not rebellion. Rest is obedience. God does not require you to carry what is crushing you to prove your faith. He invites you to lay it down and live.

Marriage should not break you more than it builds you. Staying in pain is not proof of faithfulness. Often it is proof of fear.

The Chaos of Trying to Make a Man

I tried to fix men. Somewhere I learned to believe that my love could transform another human being. If I loved hard enough, if I prayed long enough, if I gave until I was empty, surely he

46

would see my worth. Surely he would become the man I needed him to be. That belief trapped me in a cycle I could not break.

His inability to change was not about my value. I was never assigned to be his project manager. I was not responsible for molding him into a man. Women who enter relationships to fix men end up emotionally bankrupt. You cannot pour your destiny into someone and still have enough left to live.

The Psychology of "Fixing" in Relationships

Many of us step into codependent rescuing because of old wounds. If love was inconsistent in childhood, we may learn to earn it. As adults we over-function, hoping devotion will secure us a place in someone's heart. But love rooted in fixing is not love. It is control disguised as compassion. Identity built on someone else's growth leaves you depleted, while the other person remains unchanged. You cannot love a person into wholeness if they are committed to staying broken.

God Never Called Us To Be His Savior

Trying to "make a man" is spiritual warfare against your own peace. He must want transformation for himself. My belief that I could earn love nearly destroyed me. Real love is not earned. Real love is offered freely and reciprocated willingly.

Only God transforms hearts. Only God repairs what is broken inside someone. It is not our assignment to carry the weight of another person's healing.

A Warning to Women Who Are Trying To Make a Man

If you are doing all the emotional work, hoping he will change, sacrificing your peace for his potential, hear me. Stop trying to make him. Stop trying to be his everything. You deserve love that does not drain you. You deserve someone already doing the work to be whole, not someone waiting for you to do it for them.

"Not by might nor by power, but by My Spirit," says the Lord. — Zechariah 4:6

Let this be freedom for your soul. You are not his Spirit, not his Savior, and not his solution. You are God's daughter. You are worthy of love that protects your peace.

Moments of Joy in the House of God

The church has also been my sanctuary. Women prayed me through nights that felt endless. Mothers placed oil on my hands and spoke life over my children. They brought clothes and groceries when money was thin. Sisters in the choir covered me with harmony and hugs. Friends sat beside me during altar calls and did not let me stand alone. We celebrated baptisms, first Sundays, baby dedications, and quiet prayers that made me feel seen. We laughed in kitchens and shared testimonies that kept us believing. Community in God's house has been a saving grace for so many women. The church is not the villain in my story. It is a place where I learned to breathe again.

The Final Goodbye

I left Rob many times in my mind, but when I filed for divorce, a hole ripped open in my heart. Divorce brought a new level of brokenness. I never pictured myself as a divorced woman. I believed my marriage would stand the test of time. Choosing myself did not feel good at first. I questioned everything. I wondered if I made a mistake, if I should have stayed silent and endured. That was not God's will for me. I know that now, even if I could not see it then.

"So if the Son sets you free, you will be free indeed." — John 8:36

Freedom is not a rumor. Freedom is your inheritance. You are allowed to step out of what was breaking you and into what God is building in you. Forgive yourself for not knowing sooner. Bless the lessons. Walk forward.

A Prayer for Women Who Feel Trapped in a Painful Marriage

Lord, I lift every woman who feels held in a covenant that is hurting her. You know the weight she carries, the nights she cannot sleep, the questions that will not quiet down. Meet her with truth and tenderness. Remind her that she is Your daughter, not a casualty of someone else's choices. Heal the parts of her heart that have been pierced by betrayal. Where there has been confusion, give clarity. Where there has been fear, give courage. Where there has been shame, cover her with honor.

Teach her to set holy boundaries without bitterness. Teach her to forgive without returning to harm. Surround her with wise counsel, safe community, and provision for every practical need. If reconciliation would honor You and protect her, make the path unmistakably clear. If release is the door to life, open it and give her steady feet to walk through. Let her feel Your nearness, hear Your voice, and trust Your timing. Restore her joy. Restore her dignity. Restore her peace. In Jesus' name, Amen.

6

Chapter Six: Unparented: Healing the Wounds of a Mother's Pain and a Father's Absence

I was born in Mississippi to two people who were young and in love. They came from different worlds and carried different ideas about life. We left the South before I could experience a father's love and protection. My mother loved me, but she had never learned how to nurture or protect me.

As a child, I craved safety, tenderness, and presence. Instead, I met silence, survival, and emotional distance. I spent years trying to earn the love that should have been given freely. The world says to honor your parents no matter what. The truth is that some of us are grieving the loss of people who are still alive. Some of us are healing from the very hands that should have held us.

This is not about blame. It is about sharing my truth. It is about growing up unparented, carrying generational wounds, and trying to become the parent you never had. It is about facing sorrow with open eyes, telling the truth without bitterness, and building something better for the children who come after us.

The Generational Burden: My Mother's Pain Became Mine

For a long time I saw my mother only through the lens of my pain. I saw what she could not give. I felt the absence. I lived through the consequences of her choices, and anger felt easier than understanding.

Healing, growth, and motherhood taught me to see her as a woman first. A woman who was wounded and never given the tools to become whole. A woman expected to pour into me when no one ever poured into her. Before she could heal, she had me. Her life was never her own. Her trauma became my inheritance. She did not pass it down on purpose. She passed it down because no one taught her how to break it.

According to Dr. Joy DeGruy, author of Post Traumatic Slave Syndrome, many Black families carry historical trauma that has never been addressed. Our survival often came with silence, and silence became the shield that kept our mothers and grandmothers going. What protected them wounded us.

"The Lord is close to the brokenhearted and saves those who are crushed in spirit." — Psalm 34:18

God does not shame the brokenhearted. He draws near to them. That truth frees me to tell my story without dishonoring my mother. I can name what hurt and still be held by the One who saves the crushed in spirit. I can honor her humanity and honor my healing at the same time.

Honoring a Mother Who Could Not Be What I Needed

It is easy to honor a mother who loved you well. It is holy work to honor a mother who could not. Mother's Day hits like a wave. My sister and I talk about it because pretending does not feel right. Pretending we were not neglected. Pretending one day can erase decades of pain. We carry guilt and confusion. It can feel like betrayal to honor other women who mothered us. It is a heavy weight, so I challenged us to release it.

We know our mother was hurt. We are not responsible for healing what we did not break. It is okay to love our mother without obligation.

I have learned:

I do not have to pretend.

I do not have to sacrifice my peace.

I do not have to fix what I did not cause.

To the ones whose mothers are still living, yet it still feels like you do not have a mother, God sees you, and He holds you.

"Honor your father and your mother, so that you may live long in the land the Lord your God is giving you." — Exodus 20:12

Honor is not denial. Honor is not silence. Honor can look like truthful boundaries, compassion without self-betrayal, prayer without pretending, and forgiveness that frees the heart. I can grieve the mother I needed and still choose to be a different kind of mother for my children.

"He heals the brokenhearted and binds up their wounds." — Psalm 147:3

I do not need to bleed to prove I love her. I am allowed to let God bind up what was torn. Healing is not a rejection of my mother. Healing is obedience to the God who mends.

What "Present but Not Present" Felt Like

When my mother was in the house, it often felt like she was not there. I felt alone. Her body was near, while her heart was far away, hidden behind fatigue, survival, and old storms that never passed. I learned to read moods and adjust accordingly. I learned to shrink my needs so I did not add weight to her day. I became the quiet fixer, the early caregiver, the girl who knew how to sweep floors and swallow feelings.

That presence without presence shaped me. I became hyper-vigilant. I over-performed to feel safe. I confused peace with silence. I mistook love for labor. I learned to carry everyone and forgot that I was a child.

The Emotional Consequences of Growing Up Without a Father

When children grow up without a father in their lives, it can create an emotional void that shapes how they see themselves and the world. It is not simply a missing presence; it is a missing piece of identity. It can leave a child with unspoken questions that echo into adulthood. Why was I not enough to make him stay? Was it my fault? Will love always leave?

Those questions lived in me. They shaped how I loved and who I trusted. They made me reach for attention that felt like protection. They taught me to tolerate what I should have walked away from. The absence was mine, and it was common in the community around me. Not because we did not value family. Not because Black men do not love their children. A long history of oppression targeted our families and tried to fracture our bonds. Paternal absence has bled through generations of my family, including my own children.

When a father's absence met my daughters, I had no easy answers, because I had asked the same questions about my own father. The ache they felt was the ache I had carried for most of my life. This cycle of broken families was around me growing up, and it is still alive in our communities today.

From slavery to mass incarceration, Black fathers have been torn from their families through forced labor, unjust laws, and targeted policing. These are not isolated incidents. They are systemic assaults on the structure and soul of the Black family. Research from the Institute for Family Studies and the National Fatherhood Initiative shows that children raised without fathers are more likely to face poverty, drop out of school, experience early pregnancy, and encounter mental health struggles. For Black girls specifically, the absence of a father is linked to issues of self-worth, increased vulnerability to sexual exploitation, and a lifelong hunger to be chosen and protected.

"Even if my father and mother abandon me, the Lord will hold me close." — Psalm 27:10 (NLT)

When people fail me, God does not. I am held. I am not the one who was not chosen. I am the one God kept.

Finding My Father, Finding Myself

I saw my father once when I was eleven. Then there was silence for twenty-five years. As an adult I searched and found a sister on my father's side. She opened the door and helped us reconnect. Meeting him stirred hope, anger, confusion, and longing at the same time. I had kept that space locked to protect my heart.

I learned that restoration is a choice. Forgiveness can happen without reunion. You can release resentment and still guard your heart.

I chose to reconnect when I was ready. Our relationship has grown more than I expected. My children made a different choice, and I honor it. Healing is not a single path. It is a faithful one.

"Though my father and mother forsake me, the Lord will receive me." — Psalm 27:10

Even when the door I wanted stayed closed, God received me. That truth steadied my steps toward the doors I could open.

When I Was Not There

There was a season when I was physically present for my daughters and still not available to them. I was exhausted in my body, tangled in my mind, and numb in my emotions. I loved them, yet I was not there in the ways they needed. I missed their cues. I rushed their tears. I hid my own wounds and called it strength.

I have told them the truth about that season and asked for their forgiveness. I am making amends with time, attention, and tenderness. I will do everything I can to build the relationships with my Six Reasons and free us from our past.

I have learned that strong mothers are not the ones who never break. Strong mothers are the ones who repair. My daughters are my witnesses and my reasons. I am building something different with them.

Preparing Our Children in a World That Is Not Gentle

Raising Black children means teaching them how to carry truth and still keep their softness. I teach them to name what hurts and set boundaries that protect their peace. I teach them to love their people and challenge systems that harm them. I teach them that family is a circle we keep widening with safe hearts and steady hands. We use what we have. We heal what we can. We refuse to pass down what tried to master us.

Moments of Joy

Meeting my paternal siblings for the first time felt like finding pages of a story I had been reading with missing chapters. We looked at each other's faces and found familiar eyes. We shared memories that did not match and still belonged to the same book. We laughed and cried over the years we could not get back and decided to write the ones we still had.

Growing up, my maternal siblings were my first friends. We made meals out of little and joy out of less. We learned to survive together and to celebrate small wins. Protecting them flooded my soul, even when it left me wounded. They needed me, and I needed them to need me. Those moments did not erase the hurt. They gave it context. They reminded me that even in hard houses, God plants joy.

A Prayer for Mothers Breaking the Cycle

Lord, thank You for drawing near to the brokenhearted. Strengthen every mother who is choosing a new way. Lift the weight that sits on her chest. Heal what she does not have words to explain. Teach her to rest without guilt and to lead with truth and tenderness. Give her wisdom for hard boundaries and soft answers. Restore her joy. Bless her children with the security she never had. Let love be the loudest lesson in her home. Surround every child who aches with the assurance that You hold them close. Show us, generation by generation, how to repair what was torn. In Jesus' name, Amen.

Loud Truths I Learned in the Silence

Someone can give you life and not know how to love you. Your worth is not on trial.

A mother's humanity does not cancel a daughter's hurt. Both can be honored in the light.

Honor without truth is not honor. Truth without love is not healing.

Forgiveness is freedom. Reconciliation is a choice. Safety is a requirement.

Presence without presence wounds. Repair requires attention, apology, and change.

You can be the first in your line to do it differently. The cycle stops where courage begins.

God receives the abandoned, binds the wounded, and teaches us how to build again.

7

Chapter Seven: The Silence of Motherhood

Mothering in Silence

Motherhood is supposed to be a place of refuge. A place where love is given freely, where children feel safe, and where they learn their worth. But something different happens when a mother is too broken to give her children what they need. The wounds she carries become the burdens her children inherit.

For years, I thought I was protecting my children from my pain by staying silent. I thought if I did not talk about my struggles, they would not feel them. But children always know. My silence was loud. They felt my pain even when I never spoke a word about it. They carried my burdens even when I thought I was shielding them. They absorbed my suffering even when I tried to pretend it was not there. While trying to protect them, I passed down the very wounds I had never healed.

I wanted to save my children from the pain I experienced as a child. The truth is that while I was trying to build a life different from what my parents gave me, I unintentionally exposed them to traumatic experiences because I was still the unhealed child I had once been. Research from the National Child Traumatic Stress Network confirms that trauma is often passed down through behaviors, attachment patterns, and unspoken emotional wounds. In many Black families, where silence has been a survival tool, trauma can hide in plain sight for decades.

The Burden of Being "The Backbone"

The expectation to be the backbone often means Black women are seen as support systems rather than people who need support themselves. We are taught that our strength is our greatest asset. Too often it becomes our heaviest burden. The weight of always being there for others, while rarely being poured into, leads to exhaustion, emotional neglect, and even physical health issues.

This is why we see so many Black women struggling with anxiety, depression, and stress related illness. Our bodies carry what our mouths do not speak. We must shift the narrative. Black women do not just deserve rest and healing. We require it. A mother who is too depleted to care for herself cannot fully be there for her children.

Inherited Silence: The Weight We Did Not Mean to Pass Down

I wore the Strong Black Woman armor too well. It taught me how to keep going when I should have stopped. How to hold it together when I was falling apart. How to smile while I was quietly suffocating. It taught me to hide my pain, to keep my tears private, to be silent when I should have spoken. And it taught my daughters the same thing.

Before I knew it, I was walking my children through experiences I had not processed myself. My inner child was still crying

59

out. I knew if I did not face my pain, I would pass it down. I knew the cycle needed to end with me, but I did not know how to break it. No one showed me how, and the hurt kept coming.

It became clear when one of my girls said, "I learned how to hide my pain by watching you, Mom." That sentence broke me in a way I still have not fully recovered from. I did not mean to give her silence. I did not mean to pass down survival instead of softness. But I did. Now I am helping them break it.

I want my daughters to know they do not have to hide their pain or pretend. They do not have to suffer in silence. They watched me act strong because I was afraid to show my weakness. But vulnerability is not weakness. Vulnerability is an invitation to healing, to connection, to freedom. We were never meant to carry this weight alone. Women need each other. Black women need community. The world does not only need to see our strength. It needs to see our struggle, so it can witness where we found our joy. I want and need my sisters, and I will teach my daughters to build community and live connected to others instead of living in isolation.

My Six Reasons

My daughters are my six reasons. They are the reasons I got up when life knocked me down. The reasons I chose counseling, prayer, and community over silence. The reasons I learned to apologize and to start again. Each one carries light that looks a little different. One is steady and wise. One is fire and laughter. One is gentle and protects everyone else. One is bold and sees possibility in dark rooms. One is resilient and always finds her way home. One is joy that refuses to be buried. Together they are my sunrise.

Moments of Joy

Saturday mornings smelled like hair oil and warm towels. I sat each girl between my knees and parted their hair with a steady hand. The comb clicked against barrettes on the coffee table. The TV hummed with our favorite shows. We laughed at the same scenes every week. Those mornings felt like peace and routine, a rhythm that told them they belonged.

On other afternoons we turned the hallway into a runway. They slipped their feet into my heels and practiced their walk like movie stars. We clapped and cheered. They posed and twirled and fell into each other laughing. Those moments stitched beauty into hard days and taught us that joy is not something we wait for. Joy is something we make.

Scripture & Reflection

"The LORD is close to the brokenhearted and saves those who are crushed in spirit"—Psalm 34:18

God is near to the brokenhearted and saves the crushed in spirit. I am not alone in my repair. God sits with me while I heal, and my daughters are covered while I learn a new way.

"and provide for those who grieve in Zion— to bestow on them a crown of beauty instead of ashes, the oil of joy instead of mourning, and a garment of praise instead of a spirit of despair. They will be called oaks of righteousness, a planting of the Lord for the display of his splendor" —Isaiah 61:3

God exchanges ashes for beauty, mourning for gladness, heaviness for praise. What felt ruined can be restored. My home can learn a new sound. My girls can inherit my joy and assurance instead of my grief and shame.

I will repay you for the years the locusts have eaten— the great locust and the young locust, the other locusts and the locust swarm— my great army that I sent among you." —Joel 2:25

What was lost is not beyond recovery. Time was not wasted. God redeems the years, and our family story can bear new fruit.

Healing, Restoration, and Hope

Healing began when I told the truth out loud. I named the harm I survived and the harm I caused. I apologized without excuses. I asked my daughters what they needed and I listened. We created family rhythms that protect our peace. We pray. We rest. We eat together when we can. We go to therapy. We practice boundaries. We take turns being strong and we take turns being held.

Restoration looks like repair in motion. It is checking in after a hard conversation. It is circling back when my tone was sharp. It is accountability when old patterns reach for me. It is counseling to learn regulated breathing and to practice new thoughts. It is creating a village of aunties, mentors, and friends so my girls never have to search for help in the dark.

Hope looks like vision. We say what kind of women we want to be and what kind of mothers we refuse to be. We bless our bloodline with new language. We speak peace over our grandchildren. We declare that tenderness is not a luxury in our house. Tenderness is policy.

What My Daughters Face Now—and How We Stop the Spillover

My daughters are adults now. They carry adult questions. Some struggle with perfectionism because they learned that approval was safer than honesty. Some over function because they watched me carry too much. Some hold back tears because they do not want to be a burden. Some do not trust love because the people they loved the most hurt them.

We are breaking this. We name what is happening without shame. We learn to ask for help before we collapse. We practice telling the truth in real time instead of hours later. We pause when anger enters the room. We ask, what do you need right now. We choose repair over retreat.

We are teaching the next generation a new grammar. Feelings are welcome. Rest is allowed. Tears are safe here. Boundaries are love. Apologies are normal. Forgiveness is a process. Accountability is protection. Community is medicine. God is present.

Practical Rhythms for Generational Healing

Family check ins every week with three questions. What felt heavy? What felt holy? What do you need?

Repair language we can grab when emotions run high. I am sorry. I was wrong. Thank you for telling me the truth. How can I make this right?

A ritual of blessing for birthdays and milestones. We speak life over our children and remind them who they are.

Shared care. No one is the only strong one. We rotate tasks and we rotate rest.

Therapy and community. We invite wise voices to sit with us, to model soft power, to hold us accountable to our healing.

Loud Truths I Learned from the Silence

- Presence heals more than plans.
- Repair is more powerful than perfection.
- Tenderness is not weakness. Tenderness is strength under control.
- Apologies remodel a home faster than lectures ever could.
- Rest is resistance and recovery. Rest keeps love from turning into resentment.
- We break the cycle by breaking our silence. We keep it broken by practicing love in public and in private.

A Litany to Speak Over Our Daughters and Ourselves

You are not the weight you carried. You are not the words that wounded you. You are not the worst thing you survived. You are chosen. You are seen. You are safe to feel. You are strong enough to rest. You are worthy of repair. You are allowed to begin again. May the women who come from us inherit peace, tenderness, and holy joy.

8

Chapter Eight: Who Worries About the Warriors?

They call her strong because she never asks. She keeps the plates spinning, pays the cost in silence, and fixes her face before the tears can leave a trace. In the daylight she carries everyone. At night she carries herself. She is the dependable one, the steady one, the daughter no one checks on because she has taught them she does not need checking.

I know her well. She is me.

A friend once said the way my daughters stood up for me reminded him of The Woman King. He laughed and said, "You're like the Woman King, that's too much for me." I laughed too, then I thought about it. A woman warrior does not fight to prove she is unbreakable. She fights to make a home where breaking is no longer required. She trains her hands for battle and her heart for mercy. She learns when to raise a sword and when to lay it down. She holds a shield with one arm and a child with the other. She does not fight to stay in pain; she fights to cure it.

"God is our refuge and strength, an ever-present help in trouble." — Psalm 46:1

You do not have to be your own shelter. Let God be the roof and the walls while you learn to rest. Strong does not mean solitary; help is holy.

What The Woman King Taught Me About War and Healing

Sisterhood is armor. The Agojie moved as one. Strength multiplies in community. Healing does too.

A warrior can be a mother. The revelation of a mother and daughter finding each other is proof that love survives what tried to erase it.

Face the wound, then fight. Nanisca did not deny her scars. She confronted the source of her pain. She fought with rage until she found clarity. Then her reason for fighting evolved.

Discipline protects the soul. Training, boundaries, and purpose kept them from fighting every battle; they chose the battles that protected their people.

Freedom is the goal. They fought so others could live unchained. Healing is holy resistance against everything that tries to bind us.

I saw my life in those truths: the abuse, the betrayal, the ache of motherhood, the fighter in me swinging while full of pain—and then learning to fight to cure the pain. Release is not weakness; it is wisdom. Healing is not surrender; it is strategy.

"Cast all your anxiety on Him because He cares for you." — 1 Peter 5:7

You are not too much for God. Unload what you have been

carrying and let His care hold what your hands cannot.

Where I Learned to Disappear

I became the reliable one because reliability felt safer than need. Needs can be ignored. Reliability gets rewarded. In our family, survival looked like silence, and my silence was praised as maturity. I was the child who acted like a grown woman, the teenager who never asked for much, the big sister who came to the rescue, the adult who never said, "Can you hold me up?" I was the strong one. But strength without softness turns into stone. And stone sinks.

When Strength Becomes a Cage

What looked like resilience was often refusal—refusal to be a burden, refusal to need anyone. I called it boundaries; sometimes it was fear. I told myself, if I do not lean on anyone, I cannot be dropped. But the cost of doing everything alone is quiet devastation. The body keeps score when the soul is silenced. Weathering breaks us down in ways that smiling cannot cover.

"Two are better than one... If either of them falls down, one can help the other up." — Ecclesiastes 4:9–10

Falling is human; being lifted is healing. Ask someone to be your "other." Let community interrupt isolation.

Growing Up Too Soon

People saw a capable daughter and missed the child inside. The world often treats Black girls like adults before we are ready, as if we do not need protection or tenderness. When you are labeled "strong," people overlook your softness. When you are labeled "independent," people forget you are human.

God does not call you dramatic for hurting. He calls you worthy of tending. Your wounds are not proof of failure; they are places where His kindness is working.

The Bill My Body Paid

Years of high-effort coping taught me to push through fatigue and keep smiling under pressure. But unrelenting grind has a tab. Stress shows up in our blood pressure, our sleep, our breath. Pretending I did not need anyone only made it worse.

"My grace is sufficient for you, for My power is made perfect in weakness." — 2 Corinthians 12:9

Weakness is not a verdict. It is a doorway. Let grace do what grit cannot. Power flows when pretending ends.

Moments of Joy

On Sunday mornings, we sang. My girls held angelic harmony like it was stitched into their bones. We could turn anything into a song—cleaning the kitchen, folding laundry, making jokes that only we understood. We had shoobeedoop-doo-wahs with meanings no one else knew, and melodies that lifted the roof off heavy weeks. Singing was our escape and our reunion. We sang every chance we got. Those harmonies were proof that joy lives even in houses where pain tries to be loud.

Breaking the Agreement with Isolation

One day I realized I had made an agreement with isolation: I will not need anyone. I will be okay by myself. It sounded noble.

It was numbing. I started practicing a different vow: I will learn to be loved, and not just useful. I told two trusted people the truth about my capacity. I let them see the cracks behind my smile. The world did not end. I did not crumble. I began to heal.

"Carry each other's burdens, and in this way you will fulfill the law of Christ." — Galatians 6:2

Sharing weight is not weakness; it is worship. Let someone carry a bag for you. That is biblical.

What Warriors Know

1. You cannot heal what you refuse to face.

2. You cannot carry what you refuse to share.

3. You cannot protect others while abandoning yourself.

4. Discipline is a mercy; rest is a strategy.

5. Sisterhood is a shield; prayer is a weapon.

6. You fight differently when the goal is freedom, not applause.

"Come to Me, all you who are weary and burdened, and I will give you rest." — Matthew 11:28

Collapse is not the only way to stop. Choose rest before your body chooses shutdown. Trade hustle for healing, and let Jesus teach you a lighter yoke.

Loud Truths I Learned in the Silence

- Self-protection kept me alive, but connection brought me back to life.
- Being "the strong one" can become an identity that starves your soul. Retire the role.
- Asking for help is not burdening people; it is inviting love to be love.
- God does not demand performance; He desires presence.
- Rest is resistance in a world that profits from your exhaustion.
- My daughters were not just watching me fight; they were teaching me how to sing while I healed.

A Different Kind of Strength

I am still dependable. I still show up. But I want to show up as a whole woman—with needs, limits, and language. Let us practice saying: "I cannot carry that today." Let us practice receiving: "Yes, I could use a ride... a meal... a hug... a prayer." If independence has been your armor, let interdependence be your answer. Warriors do not win alone; they win together.

"The Spirit of the Lord... has sent Me to bind up the broken-hearted... to comfort all who mourn... to bestow on them a crown of beauty instead of ashes." — Isaiah 61:1–3

Beauty is not the erasure of your ashes; it is God's transformation of them. Nothing wasted. Nothing beyond redemption.

Prayer

God, I lay down the armor that kept me alive and pick up the grace that helps me live. Teach me to need without shame, to rest without guilt, and to receive without apology. Train my hands for battle and my heart for mercy. Surround me with people who lift, listen, and love like You do. Make my home a sanctuary where freedom grows. Amen.

Declaration

I am not just strong; I am supported.

I am not just capable; I am cared for.

I am not just independent; I am interdependent.

I am allowed to be held.

I am a warrior who fights to cure the pain—and to build a life where my daughters can sing in peace.

9

Chapter Nine: Learning to Love Myself Again—Healing After Betrayal and Trauma

The First Step: Admitting I Was Broken

I didn't wake up one morning knowing how to love myself. Healing did not arrive wrapped in clarity or confidence. It came slowly—through grief, trembling, and the unraveling of the image I thought was strength.

For years, I gave everything I had to everyone else. I poured love into men who didn't know how to hold it. I remained in a marriage that broke me from the inside out. I stayed loyal to churches that applauded my gifts while overlooking my soul. I kept answering the call of a mother who only wanted me when she needed me. I sacrificed myself for friendships that saw my strength but never my struggle. And I gave the little energy I had left to my beautiful children, children who needed and deserved more than I had the capacity to give. My cup had been empty for years, and I didn't even know it.

I spent my life trying to prove my worth to people who never should have had the power to question it. By the time I walked away from the pain, I didn't know who I was. In the mirror, I saw a woman betrayed, abandoned, and overlooked; a broken inner child still reaching for a mother's love; a little girl longing to be a daddy's girl; a mother grieving the moments she missed while trying to survive; a survivor of trauma too deep to speak aloud. I didn't recognize her, so I didn't know how to love her. She felt like a stranger.

Admitting I had a problem meant shattering the image others held of me. For so long, I was the strong one—the leader, the helper, the healer. I helped women and children heal from trauma. I studied the research, wrote treatment plans, led groups, helped build organizations, and created safe spaces. I assumed that helping others would heal me, too. It did not. You cannot heal what you refuse to name. You cannot pour indefinitely without running dry. I was teaching others to find freedom while living in my own cage.

Healing required me to stop hiding behind my work and take off the cape I wore so well. I had to confess that I was broken— but not beyond repair. That admission became the door. I learned that healing is not pretending you're okay; it is honoring the parts of you that aren't. It is grieving the life you should have had, forgiving what you did to survive, and learning to see your softness as sacred, not weakness.

The return to myself began quietly. I wrote letters to the little girl inside me—letters full of grace, truth, and the love she waited years to hear. I spoke her name in prayer, asking God to remind her she was never forgotten. Tears came freely, no longer blocked by shame. Rest became sacred, not selfish. Each morning, I whispered affirmations into the mirror until the woman staring back began to believe them again.

"He restores my soul; He guides me in the paths of righteousness for His name's sake." — Psalm 23:3

I am not beyond repair. God restores what life fractured. My softness is holy, my boundaries are blessed, and my healing is non-negotiable. I am worthy of care, even from me.

Healing Is Not Moving On—It's Reclaiming Yourself

For years, I believed healing meant pretending the past didn't hurt. If I smiled, produced, and kept going, maybe I could outrun the pain. Healing isn't pretending. It isn't burying the past. True healing is reclamation. It is reaching back for the parts of yourself that got lost in the chaos. It is unlearning the lies pain taught: that I was unworthy, unlovable, and too broken to be whole.

I had internalized the voices of others. I told myself I wasn't enough for real love, that I somehow deserved betrayal and abandonment, that wholeness was for other people. None of it was true. Healing began when I stopped agreeing with lies and started seeing myself the way God sees me—worthy, chosen, deeply loved.

"The Lord is close to the brokenhearted and saves those who are crushed in spirit." — Psalm 34:18

God draws near to me. I am not disqualified by my wounds. I am held, seen, and invited to rise.

Breaking Free from Shame and Guilt

Betrayal breaks more than a heart; it fractures identity. I asked myself haunting questions: Why wasn't I enough? What did I do wrong? How did I let this happen? Shame crept in like a thief, convincing me I was the problem. I blamed myself for staying, for believing words without actions, for trusting when I should have left. I carried the weight of choices made in survival—choices rooted in fear and a desperate longing to be loved.

Shame is a shapeshifter. It makes you carry what is not yours. Guilt builds a prison where you are both guard and prisoner. You replay moments. You rehearse pain. You wonder if freedom is possible.

Healing did not erase memory; it ended self-blame. Freedom began when I stopped internalizing the harm that others caused. Their actions reflected their brokenness, not my value. God never asked me to carry shame. Shame was never part of my story. Grace was.

"Those who look to Him are radiant; their faces are never covered with shame." — Psalm 34:5

"Instead of your shame you will receive a double portion... and everlasting joy will be yours." — Isaiah 61:7

Layer by layer, shame lifted. I allowed safe people to speak truth to me. I received love without suspicion. I remembered I was worthy of joy, peace, and love that does not hurt. Shame tried to silence me; grace gave me my voice back.

I am not the mistakes I made. I am not the heartbreak I endured. I am not the woman who stayed silent in her suffering. I am redeemed. I am worthy. I am whole. And so are you.

Learning to Love Myself the Way God Loves Me

The world teaches a distorted love—tied to performance, perfection, and proving. As Black women, we are told our value lives in what we do for others, not in who we are. God's love tells a different story. It is not transactional or performance-based. It is not reserved for the version of you who has it all together. God loves the real you—the you who is still healing, still learning, still crying at night, still surviving what you can barely name. He saw all of it and called you worthy.

"I have loved you with an everlasting love; I have drawn you with unfailing kindness." — Jeremiah 31:3

When I finally believed this—when I stopped hearing God through the filter of shame—I realized I didn't have to earn His love; I only had to receive it. Receiving His love changed how I loved myself. I stopped settling for crumbs and calling it a feast. I stopped shrinking in rooms I was called to lead. I stopped apologizing for my boundaries, emotions, and voice. I stopped editing myself to be palatable to those who preferred my silence. Loving myself the way God loves me meant becoming fully me—without guilt, without fear, without needing permission.

Loving Myself Means Setting Boundaries

Self-love is more than soft words and affirmations. It is fierce action. It is protection and truth-telling. It is choosing yourself even when others do not understand. For me, that began with boundaries. I had spent too long being everything for everyone—mothering grown men, repairing broken friendships alone, and staying where my peace kept being chipped away.

God never asked me to abandon myself to prove my love for

others. That is not sacrifice; that is self-neglect.

Loving myself meant:

- Saying no without over-explaining.
- Releasing people committed to misunderstanding me.
- Refusing to bleed for people who would not offer a bandage.
- Protecting my peace like my life depended on it—because it did.

"Above all else, guard your heart, for everything you do flows from it." — Proverbs 4:23

The Purpose Behind Your Pain: Breaking the Silence

Restoration is not cosmetic; it is transformational. My mother-in-law had a gift for restoring old furniture. She would find pieces that looked like junk at yard sales—scratched, chipped, wobbling, forgotten. She never saw trash; she saw potential. She scraped off the layers that didn't belong, sanded the rough places, tightened hidden screws, filled the cracks, cleansed the wood, and applied oil and stain. She worked patiently until the piece revealed its original beauty—often stronger and more valuable than before.

This is how God restores us. He does not paint over rot. He removes what cannot stay, strengthens what remains, and renews what seemed unusable. What looks like loss becomes preparation. What looks like ruin becomes revelation. The process is uncomfortable—scraping, sanding, and mending—but each pass of grace brings us closer to wholeness.

"For my thoughts are not your thoughts, neither are your ways my ways, declares the Lord." — Isaiah 55:8–9

God's vision for me is greater than what I can see. I am not discarded; I am being restored. Every scrape and sand is making me steadier, truer, and ready to carry glory without breaking.

The Power of Storytelling

Silence kept me surviving; truth started my healing process. Black women have been silenced for too long—by history, by culture, by systems, and by the fear of being disbelieved. Telling our stories interrupts the lie that pain is our destiny. It breaks generational cycles. It gives language to what our daughters feel and what our sons cannot name. Our testimony is both balm and blueprint.

Action Steps to Start Sharing Your Story

1. Name one truth you have avoided and write it in a sentence.
2. Tell it safely to a trusted friend, therapist, or women's circle.
3. Journal the impact of speaking it out loud: what felt scary, what felt freeing.
4. Choose your medium—voice note, poem, social post, prayer, or essay.
5. Set a boundary around your story: what you will share, with whom, and why.
6. Create a rhythm—ten minutes a day, once a week, or one testimony a month.
7. Celebrate the courage each time you speak, no matter how small it may seem.

Creating Safe Spaces for Black Women

- Gather circles where honesty is honored and tears are welcomed.
- Establish confidentiality and consent.
- Include rituals of care—breath-work, prayer, affirmations, and grounding.
- Invite intergenerational voices; healing multiplies when wisdom meets youth.
- Resource each other—therapists, books, crisis supports, and community aid.

Moments of Joy

Even in the thick of healing, joy kept breaking through. In the kitchen, we danced between meals, making beats on the tables and walls. In the car, we harmonized to whatever the radio handed us. Joy did not erase pain; it reminded us that God still placed light on our path.

The Journey Continues

Healing is not a destination; it is a faithful practice. Some days, the weight of the past still presses against my chest. Some days I struggle to see what God sees in me. Every day I choose to be kind to myself, to speak life, and to love myself with the same grace God gives me. I am no longer the woman who believed she wasn't enough. I am the woman who survived. I am the woman who heals. I am the woman learning—again and again—to love herself.

"So if the Son sets you free, you will be free indeed." — John 8:36

A Prayer for Those Learning to Love Themselves Again

Lord, I lift up every woman who has forgotten how to love herself. For the one who gave her all to everyone else. For the one who was taught that survival was her only option. For the one who hides her softness because the world mishandled it. Remind her she is worthy of tenderness, protection, and joy. Heal the places where betrayal cut too deep to name. Speak to the little girl inside—the one still waiting to be chosen, to be seen, to be safe. Let her tears be release, not shame. Teach her that boundaries are sacred, her voice is necessary, and her softness is divine.

Wrap her in Your love so she never forgets how You see her— whole, beloved, beautiful, and enough. When shame creeps in, drown it in grace.

In Jesus' name, Amen.

Loud Truths I Learned in the Silence

The silence I thought protected me kept me from seeing my worth.

I helped others heal while abandoning the little girl inside me; I chose to return to her—not to fix her, but to love her.

Healing is not one moment; it is the daily refusal to settle for less than what God created me to receive.

Boundaries are holy. Rest is sacred. Love does not require me to lose myself.

I am not what I survived; I am who I am becoming—and I am becoming whole.

The silence ends with me. The healing begins with me. The legacy of self-love begins here.

10

Chapter Ten: Rebuilding After the Storm—Finding Purpose in Pain

The Wounds of History and Generational Trauma

The wounds of history live in our bodies, our families, and our choices. Trauma does not vanish; it shifts and settles into the next generation unless it is named and healed. Scholars like Comas-Díaz, Hall, and Neville describe how racial trauma echoes through time in our minds and bodies. We see its imprint in the way mass incarceration fractures families, a reality documented by Western and Pettit. We see it in schools where Black children are more often policed than protected, a pattern exposed by education equity researchers. We see it in health care, where the National Academies and the CDC have called out long-standing inequities and the toll on Black mothers.

Many of us were raised where love looked like survival. Emotions felt like a luxury, and silence became a shield. We carried that shield into our relationships, our parenting, and the way we see ourselves. Healing begins when we tell the truth about these cycles and choose to break them. Youth-development and community scholars such as Shawn Ginwright call this a healing-centered approach that restores identity, imagination, and collective dignity. We can lay down survival as an identity and pick up a legacy of restoration, joy, and freedom.

Restoration Is Not Just Healing. It Is Transformation.

When something is restored, it does not simply return to what it was. It becomes stronger, more beautiful, and more useful than before.

I remember weekends with my mother-in-law at yard sales. She never knew exactly what she wanted until she saw it. She would stop at what everyone else ignored: a broken dresser, a wobbling chair, a scarred table. It looked like junk to me. To her, it was worthy. She traced the cracks with her fingers and imagined what it could become. She had a vision I could not see. This is how God sees us.

"For my thoughts are not your thoughts, neither are your ways my ways," declares the Lord. "As the heavens are higher than the earth, so are my ways higher than your ways and my thoughts than your thoughts." — Isaiah 55:8–9

God sees the finished work while you are still staring at splinters. His vision is not limited by the damage you survived. Trust the Craftsman. What people cast aside, He calls treasure, and what feels ruined becomes revelation in His hands.

Most days, I did not understand my mother-in-law's excitement. Then she began the work. The old finish came off. The broken parts were repaired. A new seal brought the grain to life. What seemed worthless became valuable and full of purpose. God does the same with us. Restoration is not only fixing what is broken; it is revealing what was always possible in God.

"Behold, I am making all things new." — Revelation 21:5

New is not a rumor over your life; it is God's agenda. Your past has no veto over your future. Walk forward. Heaven has already signed the approval for your becoming.

The Process of Restoration

1) The Scraping Away: Letting Go of What Cannot Stay
Restoration often begins with loss. Before God makes us whole, He removes what cannot remain. That looks like releasing bitterness, rejecting lies about our worth, redefining relationships that resist our healing, and laying down guilt and shame that keep us stuck. I clung to the validation of others and to an identity built around pain because I feared change would erase me. God knew that if I kept holding on, I would never step into freedom.

"Forget the former things; do not dwell on the past. See, I am doing a new thing!" — Isaiah 43:18–19

You are not obligated to keep what God is removing. Release is not failure; it is faith making room. Let go, so new life has somewhere to land.

2) The Sanding: Smoothing the Rough Edges of Our Pain
Sanding is uncomfortable. It is rough and necessary. Sanding removes what snags and splinters so the surface can receive what is new. In our lives, sanding looks like confronting pain

instead of suppressing it, allowing grief to move through us, challenging mindsets that kept us bound, and practicing self-compassion. Trauma experts like Judith Herman describe how safety, remembrance, and reconnection shape this journey, while positive-psychology researchers such as Tedeschi and Calhoun have shown how growth can emerge after deep struggle. God does not rush this work. He is careful and kind.

"Consider it pure joy, my brothers and sisters, whenever you face trials of many kinds, because you know that the testing of your faith produces perseverance." — James 1:2-3

The pressure you feel is not punishment; it is shaping. What once felt like breaking is forming the strength you will need for the next assignment. Stay on the table. God is preparing you to carry glory.

The Purpose Behind Your Pain: Breaking the Silence

For generations, Black women were told to be quiet. Endure without complaint. Carry without breaking. Suffer without sound. Silence does not heal. Silence is the prison. Our stories carry power. Health psychology research on expressive writing shows that telling the truth with structure and support can reduce distress and build meaning. And our faith teaches that testimony is a weapon.

"They triumphed over him by the blood of the Lamb and by the word of their testimony." — Revelation 12:11

Your testimony is not just survival notes; it is a key. Every time you speak truth, shame loses its grip and darkness loses ground.

Open your mouth and let freedom ring.

Taking Action: How to Begin Sharing Your Story

1. Start With Yourself

Before telling your story to others, sit with it for yourself. Journal. Pray it aloud. Notice what still aches and invite God there. Researchers who study narrative and expressive writing have long noted how this practice supports emotional regulation and meaning-making. God draws near in this honest work.

"The Lord is close to the brokenhearted and saves those who are crushed in spirit." — Psalm 34:18

You are not alone in the room with your pain. God gathers every fragment with care. He will not rush you, and He will not leave you where He found you.

2. Find a Safe Space

Not everyone can steward your story. Seek support groups, trusted friends or mentors, and faith communities that honor healing. Reviews of group-based trauma interventions show that connection reduces isolation and supports recovery when guidance is wise and culturally responsive. Scholars of religion and mental health also note that prayer, worship, and pastoral care can strengthen resilience for many Black Americans.

"Carry each other's burdens, and in this way you will fulfill the law of Christ." — Galatians 6:2

You deserve rooms where your truth is not too heavy. Community is not charity; it is covenant. Let the right people hold you while you remember how to stand.

Reclaiming Ancestral Healing Practices

Our ancestors practiced collective healing through circles of testimony, storytelling, song, food, baths, braiding, and rest. Colonization and capitalism tried to strip that away. A healing-centered lens, championed by scholars like Shawn Ginwright, calls us back to culture, imagination, and communal care. Choose spaces that honor identity and joy without performance.

3. Share in Small Steps

You do not need to tell everything at once. Share one moment, one lesson, or one scene. Write a blog post, record a video journal, or confide in a trusted friend. Small steps build a witness that strengthens you and others.

"Let the redeemed of the Lord tell their story—those he redeemed from the hand of the enemy." — Psalm 107:2

Start where your voice feels strongest. A single paragraph can open a door. A whispered truth can begin a jailbreak. Little by little becomes a legacy.

Safe Spaces for Black Women

Too often, we carry our pain alone. We are expected to be strong but not too emotional, resilient but never broken, capable but never in need. We were never meant to heal in isolation. We need spaces where we can speak without judgment, weep without labels, and tell our truth and be believed. When Black women gather in safety and faith, the world feels the tremor of our healing. God meets us there.

"Where two or three gather in my name, there am I with them."
— Matthew 18:20

When we come together, our circle becomes a sanctuary. God stands in the center and turns sorrow into strength. What tried to bury us loses its power in the presence we carry together.

Moments of Joy

Restoration is not only tears and tools. It is laughter breaking through a heavy day. It is the warm hum of the house when my girls sing on a Sunday morning. It is the clink of thrift-store finds in the trunk and the sweet talk with a mother I trust. It is pancakes flipping while music plays in the kitchen and someone starts a harmony for no reason at all. It is the first quiet breath after prayer, when peace finally sits down beside you. Joy is not a denial of pain. Joy is proof that pain does not get the last word.

Loud Truths I Learned in the Silence

- I am not what happened to me; I am what God is doing in me.
- Survival got me here. Healing will take me further.
- I can honor my past and still choose my future.
- My voice is a tool for freedom. My story is a seed for someone else's harvest.
- Community is part of my cure. Faith is part of my strategy. Joy is part of my strength.

A Prayer for Those Rebuilding After the Storm

Lord, I lift every woman stepping into her healing after the storm. Give her strength to rebuild, courage to trust again, and faith to believe in the beautiful future You have prepared. Remind her that her past does not define her and that You are making all things new. Order her steps, heal her heart, and show her how her pain is becoming purpose in Your hands. In Jesus' name, Amen.

Chapter Eleven: The Trophy of Tragedy: Breaking the Performance of Pain

The Danger of Celebrating Struggle

We have to stop treating struggle like a trophy. Strength is not endless endurance; strength is wisdom. It knows when to release, when to rest, and when to receive. True healing begins when we give ourselves permission to be soft, to be human, and to ask for help. We need more conversations that normalize Black women setting boundaries, saying no, and prioritizing peace without apology. That is the real revolution.

Retiring the Performance of Pain

Performance is the costume we put on when love has conditions. It looks like smiling through it, overworking to be worthy, telling a curated testimony instead of the truth, and becoming the "strong one" because collapse never felt safe. We start to perform to gain the attention we were denied, and we don't even know we are on stage.

Sociologist Erving Goffman called it the "presentation of self," a daily stage where we manage impressions to survive. Trauma specialists describe the fawn response—people-pleasing as protection. Scholars of the Strong Black Woman schema show how being perpetually unbreakable is praised in public, yet punishes our bodies in private. Public health research on John Henryism reveals how relentless striving against structural barriers raises stress and harms health. Somatic therapists remind us that when we perform instead of feel, the body keeps the score. The applause is loud; the cost is louder.

How Performance Steals Our Authentic Self

- It trains us to abandon our needs and seek approval instead.
- It confuses visibility with value, keeping us busy and empty.
- It turns survival skills into identity, so rest feels like failure.
- It breaks trust with the inner child, teaching her that truth is dangerous.

I know this stage well. I learned my cues, hit my marks, and called it resilience. But the curtain never closed, and my body paid the price—anxiety in my chest, sleep that would not come, a smile that hurt. I was collecting trophies for tragedy and calling it strength.

The Show Does Not Have to Go On: A Practice to Break the Act

1. Notice the cue. When you feel yourself performing—over-explaining, over-smiling, overdoing—pause. Name it: *I am performing to feel safe.*
2. Name the role. Identify which role you slipped into: *The Strong One, The Fixer, The Peacemaker, The Overachiever.*
3. Return to the body. Breathe low and slow. Unclench your

jaw. Drop your shoulders. Place one hand on your chest and one on your belly. Tell your body, *we are safe to be real.*

4. Tell one true sentence. To yourself or a trusted person: *Here is what is actually happening...* Truth breaks the spell.

5. Choose a boundary over a bow. Instead of "It's fine," say, "That hurt me. Instead of "I can do it all," say, "Here is what I can do." Instead of laughing it off, say, "I don't find this funny."

6. Find a new audience. Share your unedited story with people who can hold it. A community that requires a mask is not your community.

7. Close the curtain daily. End your day with a ritual. Write three lines: Where did I perform? What did it cost? What is one way I will practice honesty tomorrow? Then say aloud, The show is over. I choose truth.

Curtain Call

- I am worthy without a performance.
- My truth is more powerful than my image.
- I do not trade authenticity for approval.
- The curtain can close; my life goes on.
- I am safe to be seen as I am.

Moments of Joy

Laughing mid-story and letting the tears come without apology.

Saying "no" and feeling my nervous system settle.

Resting without earning it first.

Loud Truths I Learned in the Silence

- Performance is protection that became a prison.
- Applause cannot heal what honesty will.
- The self I performed is not the self I am.
- Freedom requires truth more than talent.
- Today, I retire the trophy of tragedy.

When You Get Tired of Bondage

There comes a moment when the weight of the chains is no longer bearable. You get tired of being silenced. You get tired of shrinking to make others comfortable. You get tired of surviving instead of thriving. You get tired of watching the next generation inherit cycles of pain. In that moment, you remember freedom is your birthright. You stop waiting for permission. You demand it. You fight for it. You walk in it.

"It is for freedom that Christ has set us free. Stand firm, then, and do not let yourselves be burdened again by a yoke of slavery." — Galatians 5:1

Holding On Made Me Sick

I held the pain so tightly that my body started to carry it for me. Headaches that would not release. A stomach clenched like a fist. Nights without sleep. A heart racing in empty rooms. Smiles that hurt because they were heavy with pretense. I called it strength. It was not strength. It was sickness. My body kept the score of every betrayal, every silence, every time I swallowed my voice to keep the peace. The person who hurt me never apologized. They may never apologize. I am done waiting. My healing is not a payment they can make. My healing is freedom for me.

Becoming the Woman My Younger Self Needed

I asked myself a question that I hope you will consider. Would my younger self feel safe with me? Safe enough to cry. Safe enough to tell the truth. Safe enough to be messy and still be loved. Freedom for me is becoming that woman—the one who protects the little girl inside me, listens to her, believes her, and refuses to trade her safety for anyone else's comfort.

Freedom Is Collective

Choosing freedom is not only personal; it is communal. It is for every Black woman who was told to be quiet. It is for every little girl who deserves to grow up without chains. It is for the generations who will come after us. When one of us breaks free, we clear a path for others. This is why we cannot afford to stay bound. We are fighting for our daughters to know their worth, for our sons to see Black women walk in power, and for a future where we pass down healing instead of harm.

"The Spirit of the Lord is on me, because he has anointed me to proclaim good news to the poor. He has sent me to proclaim freedom for the prisoners and recovery of sight for the blind, to set the oppressed free." — Luke 4:18

Breaking Generational Chains

For too long, I carried my mother's wounds and my grand-mother's silence. The chains that bound them tried to bind me: the silence, the suffering, the belief that endurance is love. The chains break with me. I refuse to pass down the fear of using my voice, the lie that love must hurt, or the idea that survival is enough. I choose healing so my children are not asked to carry what was never theirs.

93

"You will know the truth, and the truth will set you free." — John 8:32

The Role of Faith in Freedom

Freedom is not only letting go. It is trusting that what is ahead is greater than what is behind. For years, I felt unworthy of joy. I worried that if I let my guard down, pain would return. I wondered if God truly had better for me. Faith taught me this: I do not have to protect myself alone because God is my protector. I do not have to fight to prove my worth because God already calls me worthy. I do not have to hold pain to stay strong because God restores what was lost.

Choosing Freedom Means Leaving the Chains Behind

To walk in freedom, I leave behind guilt that said I did not deserve it, shame that told me I was still broken, and fear that whispered bondage was safer. I refuse to let the past define me, pain hold me hostage, or the world tell me who I am. I step into the life God has called me to live because I was never created for chains.

"So if the Son sets you free, you will be free indeed." — John 8:36

Freedom Requires a Daily Commitment

Every day, I choose freedom again. Some days, the past tries to call me back. Some days, fear argues that I am asking for too much. Still, I stand in what God has already declared. I am free, and I will not return to bondage.

Healing is a Community Issue: Black Men Must Heal Too

Healing is not a woman's assignment; it is a community mandate. Unhealed trauma in men often spills into the lives of women and children. The work begins with honest self-examination. It looks like listening without defense, naming and rejecting misogyny, uplifting Black women's voices, and creating safe spaces for us to be our whole selves. When Black men heal, Black families heal. When Black women are supported, entire communities thrive.

Speak Life

- I am no longer bound to what tried to break me.
- My body is a temple of healing, not a vault for pain.
- I choose peace over performance, truth over silence, and love over fear.
- I am the woman my younger self can trust.
- God restores, and I receive.

Loud Truths I Learned in the Silence

- Freedom is a choice I make daily.
- Pain held too long becomes illness. I release it.
- Apologies may never come. My healing does not wait for them.
- Survival is not the goal. Wholeness is.
- Love that requires my silence is not love.

Declaration: I Choose Freedom

I am no longer bound.

I refuse to carry chains that are not mine.

I will not apologize for choosing peace, joy, and wholeness.

I will walk in the freedom God has given me. I was made to be free.

"'For I know the plans I have for you,' declares the Lord, 'plans to prosper you and not to harm you, plans to give you hope and a future.'" — Jeremiah 29:11

A Prayer for Those Ready to Walk in Freedom

Lord, I lift every woman stepping into her freedom. Remind her she is no longer bound by her past, her pain, or the weight of other people's expectations. Give her courage to walk boldly in the life You planned for her. Let joy, peace, and wholeness rise in her like the morning. Teach her to trust You with what she releases and with what You restore.

And Lord, we lift up the men who stand beside her. We lift her brothers, fathers, uncles, cousins, partners, sons, friends, supervisors, and coworkers. Heal him at the root. Unravel the trauma he learned to carry in silence. Break the cycles that taught him to harden his heart. Give him language for his pain, a community for his healing, and the humility to listen without defense. Form in him a love that protects without control, leads with gentleness, and honors Black women as image-bearers of God. Strengthen his mind, cleanse his memories, steady his hands, and anoint his steps so he walks in freedom. Let his healing bless households, restore families, and rebuild our communities. Do not allow his trauma to become hers; make his transformation a covering, not a burden.

Seal their lives with your wisdom and peace. Let freedom be their daily choice and their steady testimony. In Jesus' name, Amen.

12

Chapter Twelve: No Longer the Villain.

Silence taught me to survive. Freedom taught me to live.

There was a season when every wound had a name and every name felt powerful. The betrayals, the absences, the hands that should have held me and did not became the villains of my story. The hardest truth I had to face was this. When pain stayed unhealed, I began to act like the villain in my own life. I was guarded when I needed to be open. I was harsh when I longed to be soft. I was quiet when my voice could have saved me. I was not evil. I was exhausted, armored, and afraid. The storm outside had passed, but the storm inside was still raging.

My own emotional reactions to the storms of life rose up to be the worst villain in our lives. I knew from experience that if I clutched fear, shame, and rage long enough, they would squeeze the life out of me. I had to learn a new way. I had to face the inner storm without becoming it. I had to tell the truth about what hurt without letting it harden me. I had to stop rehearsing the wound and begin releasing it. I wanted to let God lead me and not continue to be imprisoned by fear.

"For those who are led by the Spirit of God are the children of God. The Spirit you received does not make you slaves so that you live in fear again. Rather, the Spirit you received brought about your adoption to sonship." — Romans 8:14-15

You are not a slave to your story. You are a child of God who is led into freedom. Your past can inform you, but it cannot define you. The Spirit within you breaks every agreement with fear and invites you to walk as the beloved. Choose freedom again today. Choose it when the memories rise. Choose it when your voice shakes. Choose it because love already chose you.

When the Storm Inside Feels Bigger Than the Mountain Ahead

There were days when the obstacle in front of me looked impossible to move. Yet the loudest opposition did not always stand outside of me. It was the voice inside that said, You are too broken to try. Sit down. Be quiet. Do not risk it. Healing turned when I decided to tell the truth to myself. I was not the villain, and I was not the victim anymore. I was the narrator. I could tell a larger story where pain does not get the last word and fear does not drive the plot.

That choice required more than grit. It required vulnerability. Vulnerability is the courage to step forward with uncertainty and emotional exposure while still choosing connection and growth. It is holy bravery. It creates room for God and community to meet us where we are and carry us where we are called to go.

Breaking Free from the Villains Outside and Within

Some people must be forgiven, and some boundaries must be built. There is another practice that changes everything. I learned to externalize the problem. I stopped saying, I am angry, and started saying, Anger is visiting me. The moment I named the struggle outside my identity, I had room to fight it with wisdom instead of shame. This is the work of rewriting. My problems are not my personhood. I can reclaim the meaning of my experiences and step back into agency.

Power in Action: A Rewriting Guide

1. Name the villain accurately. Describe the behavior or belief, such as control, shame, or scarcity. Do not label yourself.
2. Track the exceptions. Notice moments when you resisted the pattern, even for a few minutes. Small victories are real doors.
3. Rewrite the scene. Ask, if love holds the pen, how does this chapter end? Then take one small aligned action today.
4. Invite a witness. Tell a trusted sister or your therapist what you are rewriting. Healing multiplies when it is seen.

Resilience Without Armor

We have been told to strap up our boots and keep going. True resilience does not look like endless grind or silent endurance. True resilience is flexible strength that grows through connection, wellness practices, meaning-making, honest thinking, restoration, and rest. Rest is not a reward. Rest is a requirement for healing. Grief is not a setback. Grief is a step in the process. Permission to be human is not a luxury. It is the doorway to wholeness.

Rest is not quitting. Tears are not weakness. Pausing is not failure. Sometimes the bravest act is to lay down the armor that no longer serves you and let your heart breathe again.

Therapy, Faith, and Sisterhood: Our Healing Ecosystem

My freedom did not come from a single altar call or one counseling session. It came from an ecosystem that included therapy, faith, healthy connections, and sisterhood over time. Therapy gave me language. Faith gave me an anchor and hope. Healthy connections gave me accountability. Sisterhood gave me a mirror and a net. When therapy honors our culture and our spirituality, it becomes a safe place to process trauma, dismantle internalized oppression, and redefine strength. The Black church has long been a refuge and a rallying point for liberation. When we weave these threads together with care, we make a covering strong enough to hold our healing.

Because Black women carry layered burdens, we need resources made for us and led by us. We deserve spaces that honor our language, our songs, our grief rituals, and our joy. Seeking help is not betrayal of our strength. Seeking help is legacy work for our daughters and their daughters.

Your Story Heals You and Us

We overcome by the blood of the Lamb and by the word of our testimony. When we tell the truth, shame loses oxygen and someone else finds a map out. Research shows that giving language to hard experiences can help many people make meaning and move pain through the body and mind over time. The results are not identical for everyone, but the practice matters. Storytelling in a safe community brings light to places that secrecy keeps dark.

Vulnerability does not oppose strength. Vulnerability births it. When we speak honestly in the right places, we open doors to connection, creativity, and change.

Power in Action: Share to Heal Safely

1. Write a one-page testimony about a moment you survived. Add one sentence of meaning that you are claiming from it.
2. Share it with one safe person or your therapist. Let empathy meet your story.
3. Ask yourself who might need to hear this so they can believe they will make it too. Protect your boundaries and the privacy of others while you share.

Freedom Is a Daily Choice

Freedom is not a trophy. Freedom is a practice. Some days it sings in your bones. Other days, you choose it with trembling hands. On both days you are free.

"It is for freedom that Christ has set us free. Stand firm then." Galatians 5:1

You are authorized to live free. Stand firm in truth, not denial. Stand firm with therapy appointments on your calendar, with boundaries that guard your peace, with joy protected, and with a circle of sisters who tell you the truth in love. Freedom is not only what God does for you. Freedom is what God cultivates within you.

Reflection and Practice

1. Tell the truth. Where have you cast yourself as a villain or a victim? What new role is God inviting you to play?
2. Name the storm. Which emotion tries to take over? Is it

fear, anger, shame, or scarcity? How will you externalize it this week?

3. Choose one step. What single action will align you with freedom today? Will you rest? Will you call your therapist? Will you set a boundary? Will you share a testimony in a safe space?

Loud Truths I Learned in the Silence

1. Silence does not protect me. Silence imprisons me.
2. My pain lives in my story, but it does not get to author it.
3. I am no longer the villain. I am the narrator, and I am a vessel.
4. Vulnerability is a doorway and not a trap. I will walk through it.
5. Freedom is a practice that I choose, guard, and share.

Prayer

Father, thank You for adopting me into freedom. Break every agreement I have made with fear, shame, and survival that keeps me small. Teach me to lay down the armor that no longer serves me and to pick up courage, truth, and love. Heal the storm within me and give me wisdom to set holy boundaries without. Anoint my story and sanctify my testimony so that it becomes medicine for me and hope for others. Surround me with therapists, pastors, brothers, and sisters who hold me accountable to wholeness.

Today I forgive myself. I forgive myself for what I did in fear and for what I failed to do in love. I release perfectionism, self-punishment, and the need to relive the scene to pay a debt You already canceled. I receive Your pardon and I agree with Your mercy. Teach me how to make amends where I can, to repair what is repairable, and to walk in restored integrity. I thank You for permission to forgive me. You have freed me from the guilt, blame, and shame I have held on to. By Your Spirit, I refuse to live as a villain or a victim. I choose to live as Your daughter, free indeed.

13

Chapter Thirteen: Lay It Down and Live: The Power of Release

Silence That Kills

Unforgiveness was poisoning me from the inside out. I carried it like a secret sickness, not realizing how deeply it was destroying me. It raised my blood pressure. It kept me awake at night. It hardened my heart. It left wounds so deep only God could heal.

Then one day it put me in a hospital bed. I lay there, unable to move my arm and leg, wondering if this was it—if this was how my story would end. Unforgiveness handed stress all the ammunition it needed to take me out.

"A heart at peace gives life to the body, but envy rots the bones."
— Proverbs 14:30

Peace is medicine. I release the person, the moment, and the memory that tried to own my body. I choose peace to flow through my mind, my breath, and my blood. I am not what happened to me. I am who God is healing me to be.

The Deadly Weight We Carry

Stress does not just weigh on the heart. It breaks the body. For many Black women, chronic stress is layered with unhealed trauma, generational grief, silencing our struggles, spiritualized endurance without rest, microaggressions and racism, the pressure to be "the strong one," and the invisible labor of caregiving. This strain shows up as high blood pressure, heart disease, stroke, autoimmune disorders, anxiety, and depression.

Being the "strong one" was killing me. Psychologists call this the Strong Black Woman schema. Over time, constant strain creates allostatic load—the body's wear and tear—and, under racism, becomes weathering, which scholars say accelerates health problems. I felt it in my own body: the pressure, the sleepless nights, the numbness I tried to pray away. My body was telling the truth long before I did.

Strength is not only endurance. Strength is knowing when to release, when to rest, and when to receive. Healing begins when we give ourselves permission to be soft, to be human, and to ask for help. We must normalize Black women setting boundaries, saying no, and prioritizing peace without guilt. That is the real revolution.

Forgiveness work has been linked to lower blood pressure and stress reactivity, less rumination and hostility, calmer heart rate, better sleep, and lighter moods. This is not excusing harm. It is refusing to let harm live in our cells.

"Come to me, all you who are weary and burdened, and I will give you rest." — Matthew 11:28

Rest is holy. I lay down what is not mine to carry. I trade the weight of bitterness for the yoke of Christ. My nervous system can learn safety again. God meets me in my breath.

What Forgiveness Does Not Mean

Forgiveness does not mean you forget what happened, reconcile with the person, or allow repeat access to your life. Forgiveness releases their grip on your heart. It chooses peace over pain. It breaks emotional chains that keep you bound to the past. It heals—even when no apology comes. Research shows release reduces rumination—the mental replay that keeps wounds open—and supports healthier sleep and mood.

"And when you stand praying, if you hold anything against anyone, forgive them, so that your Father in heaven may forgive you your sins." — Mark 11:25

I forgive to be free. I forgive to breathe. I forgive to make room for joy. My forgiveness is worship and a boundary for my future.

"And when you stand praying, if you hold anything against anyone, forgive them, so that your Father in heaven may forgive you your sins." — Mark 11:25

I forgive to be free. I forgive to breathe. I forgive to make room for joy. My forgiveness is worship and a boundary for my future.

When There's No Apology

Some who hurt me never said sorry. Some never admitted what they did. Some still believe they were right. I once thought I could not move until they acknowledged my pain. Waiting for an apology kept me trapped in yesterday. Healing is not dependent on them. Healing is a covenant between me and God.

"Do not repay anyone evil for evil... If it is possible, as far as it depends on you, live at peace with everyone." — Romans 12:17–18

My destiny is not hinged to anyone's honesty. I release them. I choose my life.

Forgiveness With Boundaries

I have forgiven people I will never let back into my life. Forgiveness must walk with wisdom. If someone shows you they do not respect you, continue to harm you, or refuse to change, you are not required to remain in the relationship. You can love from a distance. You can pray without offering access. You can forgive without returning to dysfunction.

"Above all else, guard your heart, for everything you do flows from it." — Proverbs 4:23

My heart is holy ground. I set a gate around it. God is the keeper of my boundaries, and I agree with His wisdom.

Letting Go Without Losing Yourself

I once believed forgiveness meant acting like everything was fine, going back to how it was, pretending the pain did not change me. The truth is different. Forgiveness does not erase growth. The betrayal changed me. The hurt shaped me. The lessons made me wise. I will not abandon myself to keep others comfortable.

"The Lord is close to the brokenhearted and saves those who are crushed in spirit." — Psalm 34:18

God meets me in the broken places and makes me whole. I keep the wisdom, not the wound.

Freedom: Personal and Collective

Freedom is not a faraway destination. It is a daily choice. After you have been bound too long, not choosing freedom is no longer an option. When you are tired of bondage, you stop asking permission to be free. You stand up, speak up, and walk forward.

"It is for freedom that Christ has set us free. Stand firm then, and do not let yourselves be burdened again by a yoke of slavery." — Galatians 5:1

Christ opened the door. I refuse to live like the lock is still on it. I will not pick up chains God already cut.

Freedom is not only personal. It is collective. Choosing freedom is for every Black woman told to be quiet, for every girl who deserves to grow up without chains, for every generation after us. When one of us breaks free, the path widens for all of us.

"The Spirit of the Lord is on me... to proclaim freedom for the prisoners... to set the oppressed free." — Luke 4:18

The Spirit of God rests on me for a purpose. My story announces freedom wherever I go.

Breaking generational chains means I refuse to pass down the fear of using my voice, the lie that love must hurt, or the belief that survival is enough. I choose wholeness, so my children never carry what was never theirs.

"You will know the truth, and the truth will set you free." — John 8:32

I tell the truth about what hurt me and the truth about how God is healing me. Truth breaks chains in my bloodline.

Freedom Requires a Daily Commitment

Some days the past pulls. Some days fear speaks. Some days the world calls me too much. Every day I return to the truth that God has already set me free. Some of us survived by outworking the pain. That high-effort coping has a name— John Henryism—and it can raise blood pressure when support is scarce. Choosing freedom means refusing to grind yourself into the ground to prove you're okay. Self-compassion is not indulgence; research links it to steadier sleep, better nourishment, more movement, and lower stress. That is stewardship of the life God entrusted to me.

"So if the Son sets you free, you will be free indeed." — John 8:36

Jesus secured my freedom. My emotions may shift, but my status remains the same. I am free indeed.

Moments of Joy

After I released what tried to bury me, simple things became holy again. Joy returned in ordinary ways. It did not ask for permission. It came because I finally made room. Release and make room for the joy you deserve. Clear the clutter pain left behind so joy has space to reside.

Loud Truths

- Unforgiveness is a thief. It steals rest, joy, and years.
- Forgiveness is not reconciliation. Boundaries are biblical and necessary.
- Your body keeps the score. Release is a health practice, not just a feeling.
- You can honor your story without replaying your pain.
- Freedom is not accidental. It is a daily choice—for you and the generations watching you.

A Healing Practice: Forgive Without Forgetting Yourself

1. Breathe and Name: Hand over heart. Inhale four, exhale six. Name the hurt out loud.
2. Release and Retain: Write one sentence that releases the person, and one that retains the lesson. Keep the lesson. Burn the hurt.
3. Bless and Block: Pray a blessing over their life. Then write one boundary that protects yours.
4. Move the Body: Take a 10-minute walk. Let your steps preach: *I am moving forward.*
5. Return to Rest: Before bed, repeat, "I release you. I choose peace," until sleep finds you.

A Prayer for Those Ready to Forgive and Walk Free

Lord, You see every woman who has carried wounds for

years. You know the sleepless nights, the clenched jaw, the smile that hid a storm. Today, we refuse to live as hostages to what happened. We place the hurt in Your hands. Break our agreements with bitterness and avenge us with healing, not harm.

Give us courage to release what poisons us and the wisdom to keep holy boundaries. Restore what trauma tried to take—our breath, our rest, our joy. Teach our bodies safety again. Make forgiveness our warfare and freedom our portion. Let truth cut the chains, let peace guard our hearts, and let joy take up residence in our homes. We choose life. We choose peace. We choose You. In Jesus' name, Amen.

A Declaration for the Free

I am no longer bound.
I refuse to carry chains that were never mine.
I will not apologize for choosing peace, joy, and wholeness.
I walk in the freedom God has given me—today and every day.

14

Chapter Fourteen: Walking in Wholeness and Leaving a Legacy

Breaking the Cycle! It Stops Here!

For generations, we carried burdens that were never meant to be ours. We inherited silence, passed down pain, and were expected to endure what should have broken us. The cycle can stop here. We are the ones who say, no more.

No more suffering in silence.

No more passing down trauma as if it were an inheritance.

No more believing that survival is the best we can hope for.

We are the ones who choose to heal, not only for ourselves but for our children and for every generation that follows. Healing is a legacy, and the way we choose to heal will shape the future.

"The Lord will fight for you; you need only to be still." — Exodus 14:14

The Weight of Legacy: What Will You Pass Down?

We are not only healing for ourselves. We are healing for those who come after us. We are healing for our daughters so they never question their worth. We are healing for our sons so they learn to honor and uplift Black women. We are healing for our families so the cycles of trauma and silence are broken for good. We are healing for every little girl who comes after us so she never wonders if she is loved, seen, or enough.

The world tried to silence us for too long. Our voices, our healing, and our freedom are our inheritance. We will pass down strength, wisdom, love, and healing.

"A good person leaves an inheritance for their children's children." — Proverbs 13:22

The Power of Breaking Generational Curses

Pain, trauma, and silence are not legacies. They are chains. When we heal, we break every single one. Every prayer we pray matters. Every truth we speak matters. Every choice to choose healing over hurt rewrites our family's history.

Our healing lays the foundation for something new. A new story. A new legacy. A new future where our children do not have to heal from the same wounds we carried.

"You intended to harm me, but God intended it for good to accomplish what is now being done, the saving of many lives." — Genesis 50:20

Healing Is an Act of Resistance

Black women have carried the weight of the world on our backs. We were told to be strong, to endure without complaint, and to keep our pain private.

Healing refuses that assignment. Healing says, I will not carry this weight any longer. Healing says, I will not pass this pain to my children. Healing says, I will not accept suffering as my destiny.

Choosing healing is choosing yourself. Choosing healing is choosing freedom. Choosing healing is choosing legacy.

"Instead of your shame you will receive a double portion, and instead of disgrace you will rejoice in your inheritance. And so you will inherit a double portion in your land, and everlasting joy will be yours." — Isaiah 61:7

Creating a Path for Future Generations

The road we walk now paves the way for those who come next. One day, our children will look back and see the sacrifices we made. They will know that we chose to heal so they would not have to carry our wounds. They will know that we chose to speak so they would not suffer in silence. They will know that we broke cycles so they could walk free.

Our healing is a bridge. It carries us from a past that hurt us into a future that heals them. The most powerful thing we can do is keep walking forward.

"Do not be conformed to this world, but be transformed by the renewing of your mind." — Romans 12:2

Your Story Is Not Over — It Is Just Beginning

If you take nothing else from this journey, take this truth. You are not bound by your past. You are not limited by what happened to you. You are not defined by your wounds. You are free. You are healed. You are walking in a new legacy of wholeness.

"And I will restore to you the years that the locust has eaten."
— Joel 2:25

Speak Life

I am the ending of what tried to end me.
I am the beginning of healing in my family.
I choose peace, and peace chooses me.
I choose truth, and truth makes me free.
I carry wisdom, not wounds.
I carry faith, not fear.
God restores my years and multiplies my joy.
Wholeness is my portion.
Freedom is my inheritance.
Legacy is my gift to the generations.

A Final Prayer for Wholeness and Legacy

Lord, we thank You for every woman who has walked these pages with courage, honesty, and hope. Thank You for meeting her in the deep places and for proving that nothing is beyond Your power to heal. Breathe peace into the rooms that once held pain. Breathe strength into the places that felt empty. Breathe purpose into every step she takes from this day forward.

Restore what was lost and redeem what was broken. Uproot every lie that told her she was not enough. Plant truth where shame once grew. Crown her with wisdom and surround her with people who speak life. Let her body, mind, and spirit agree with Your promise of wholeness. Let the oil of joy run over every scar and turn every wound into a well of compassion and strength.

Give her the courage to forgive others and the grace to forgive herself. Release her from guilt, blame, and regret. Teach her to rest in Your love without apology. Teach her to guard her heart with holy boundaries. Teach her to stand in her freedom with a steady voice and a steady mind.

Bless the generations that come from her. Let her daughters know their worth and walk in unshakable dignity. Let her sons honor Black women and rise as protectors, builders, and peacemakers. Heal families. Heal marriages. Heal communities. Break the silence that has lingered for too long and replace it with testimonies that set others free.

Anoint her legacy. Let her home become a sanctuary of laughter, learning, and love. Let her work carry healing into the streets and into the systems that once harmed her. Open doors she could not open on her own. Close the doors that threaten her peace. Order her steps and give her divine strategy to sustain what You have restored.

God, let her know that this is not the end of her story. This is the unveiling of who she truly is in You. Make her a living memorial of Your faithfulness. Make her name a blessing that echoes through her children's children. Let freedom be her family's language. Let wholeness be their way of life. Let joy be their daily song.

We seal this prayer in the name of Jesus. Amen.

15

References

Aughinbaugh, A., Robles, O., & Sun, H. (2013). Marriage and divorce: Patterns by gender, race, and educational attainment. Monthly Labor Review, 136(10), 1–16. https://doi.org/10.21916/mlr.2013.32

Biblica. (2011). Holy Bible: New International Version (NIV). Biblica.

Burton, L. M., & Tucker, M. B. (1999). Black marriage patterns: Representations and realities. In M. Lamont (Ed.) The cultural territories of race: Black and White boundaries (pp. 204–218). University of Chicago Press.

Comas-Díaz, L., Hall, G. N., & Neville, H. A. (2019). Racial trauma: Theory, research, and healing. American Psychologist, 74(1), 1–16. https://doi.org/10.1037/amp0000442

Centers for Disease Control and Prevention. (2024). Pregnancy Mortality Surveillance System. Author. https://www.cdc.gov/reproductivehealth/maternal-mortality/pregnancy-mortality-surveillance-system.htm

Epstein, R., Blake, J. J., & González, T. (2017). Girlhood interrupted: The erasure of Black girls' childhood. Georgetown

Law Center on Poverty and Inequality. https://genderjusticean dopportunity.georgetown.edu/wp-content/uploads/2020/06/g irlhood-interrupted.pdf

Ginwright, S. A. (2018, May 31). The future of healing: Shifting from trauma-informed care to healing-centered engagement. Medium. https://medium.com/@ginwright/the-future-of-hea ling-shifting-from-trauma-informed-care-to-healing-cente red-engagement-634f557ce69c

H.E.R. (2021). For Anyone [Song] On Back of My Mind. RCA Records.

Healthy Marriage and Responsible Fatherhood. (n.d.). Marriage and divorce statistics by culture: African Americans and Black community. National Healthy Marriage Resource Center. https://www.healthymarriageinfo.org/research-policy/marria ge-facts-and-research/marriage-and-divorce-statistics-by-culture/african-americans-and-black-community/

Herman, J. L. (2015). Trauma and recovery: The aftermath of violence—from domestic abuse to political terror (Rev. ed.). Basic Books.

Hunter, T. W. (2017). The history of Black marriage https://te rawhunter.com/the-history-of-black-marriage/

Kreider, R. M., & Ellis, R. (2011). Marriage and divorce patterns by gender, race, and educational attainment. U.S. Census Bureau. https://www.bls.gov/opub/mlr/2013/article/marriage-and-div orce-patterns-by-gender-race-and-educational-attainment. htm

Livingston, G., & Brown, A. (2017, June 12). Key facts about race and marriage 50 years after Loving v. Virginia. Pew Research Center. https://www.pewresearch.org/short-read s/2017/06/12/key-facts-about-race-and-marriage-50-years-after-loving-v-virginia/

Morris, M. W. (2016). Pushout: The criminalization of Black girls in schools. The New Press.

National Academies of Sciences, Engineering, and Medicine. (2020). Birth settings in America: Outcomes, quality, access, and choice. The National Academies Press.

National Black Women's Justice Institute. (n.d.). Fact sheet: Sexual abuse and assault of Black girls and women. Author. https://www.nbwji.org

National Fatherhood Initiative. (2023). Father Facts (9th ed.). National Fatherhood Initiative.

Pettit, B., & Western, B. (2018). Mass incarceration and racial inequality. Annual Review of Criminology, 1, 151–171. https://doi.org/10.1146/annurev-criminol-032317-091915

Potter, H. (2018). Understanding the role of marriage in Black women's lives: An exploration of commitment, loyalty, and trust. Race and Justice, 8(4), 356–375. https://doi.org/10.1177/2153368718772701

Prince-Bythewood, G. (Director). (2022). The Woman King [Film]. TriStar Pictures.

Raley, R. K., Sweeney, M. M., & Wondra, D. (2015). The growing racial and ethnic divide in U.S. marriage patterns. The Future of Children, 25(2), 89–109. https://www.jstor.org/stable/43581971

Tyndale House Publishers. (2015). Holy Bible: New Living Translation (NLT). Tyndale House Publishers.

Tedeschi, R. G., & Calhoun, L. G. (2004). Posttraumatic growth: Conceptual foundations and empirical evidence. Psychological Inquiry, 15(1), 1–18. https://www.jstor.org/stable/20447194

U.S. Bureau of Labor Statistics. (2024, September). Patterns of marriage and divorce from ages 15 to 55: Evidence from the